SCHOOL DAZE

THE HINKLEY COMMUNITY
COLLEGE CHRONICLES

CRAIG SULLIVAN

Llumina
Press

Requests for permission to make copies of any part of this work should be mailed to Permissions Department, Llumina Press, 7580 NW 5th Street #16535 Plantation, FL 33318.

ISBN: 978-1-62550-309-1

Printed in the United States of America by Llumina Press

Library of Congress Control Number: 2015913471

AUTHOR NOTE:

This story is fiction. All names, locations, and general descriptions were inspired by the imagination of the author. Any recognizable name or place is either a nationally renowned person or place or merely coincidental and not intentional.

PROLOGUE

Dr. Ramblewood gave the microphone positioned in front of him a light rap, making sure the amplification system was working and hoping to bring the modest crowd to attention. Tall, slight of build, wearing a tweed sport coat with leather patches on the elbows, Ramblewood exuded intellectual superiority. His stature was further accentuated by wire rim reading glasses perched on his long nose and lassoed to his neck by a fine silver chain. His meticulously colored fine hair left only a hint of grey over his ears and his closely trimmed goatee expressed impeccable grooming detail.

Ramblewood glanced to his right, making subtle eye contact with Dr. Mahaylia Busch, confirming she was ready to begin the proceedings, and did the same in the opposite direction, giving a slight tilt of his head to Dr. Winslow Burpee, the third member of the Community College Resource Accreditation and Performance Board, commonly referred to as CRAP.

Ramblewood thumped the microphone. "Can everyone hear me? We would like to get started now if you'll take your seats."

A few of the small assembled group moved toward open seats, creating screeches and unsettling racket as chairs were moved and oriented on the cement floor. Others ignored the request and continued to sip coffee and munch on the selection of pastries provided by the students enrolled in the Creative Culinary Skills class hoping for a Certificate of Learning in restaurant management.

Ramblewood moved closer the microphone, made a show of looking at his watch and added some attitude to his plea. "Folks, we would like to get started so we can stick to our agenda. We have a lot to cover today........" (Thump, thump, thump). "Can everyone hear me?"

Dr. Busch loudly exhaled with frustration like a breaching humpback, and without rising, leaned over and reached for the microphone. At four hundred pounds, trying to rise from her chair would put severe strain on her pucker power, given the gastric distress she was currently suffering, so she slid the microphone as close as the wire feed would allow and shouted, "Alright people, put the freaking coffee down and find a seat. This isn't a social hour."

Ramblewood cleared his throat maintaining his cool and collected persona and scooted the microphone back. "Uh, thank you Dr. Busch. This meeting of the Illinois Community College Resource Accreditation and Performance Board is called to order." He put his hand across his forehead to shield his eyes and searched the audience. "Reverend, are you out there? Reverend Smith? Ah, there you are. Reverend Smith of the Hinkley Unity Cultural Center will give us an invocation."

Reverend Smith dressed in a floral open collar shirt, Croc open towed sandals, hoop ear rings and a braided pony tail, maneuvered through the crowd and positioned himself in front of the elevated stage. "Oh holy one, father of Jesus, Mohammad, Buddha and a host of other profits, bless this proceeding and allow our community college to continue to offer spiritual and educational guidance to the mere mortals that temporarily inhabit your earth. We ask this blessing in a general way so as not to offend. Amen."

"Thank you Reverend Smith for those encouraging…….. For that……., prayer, I guess." Ramblewood adjusted his coat sleeves and rested his elbows on the table drawing closer to the microphone. "Well, I guess we will get started. Thank you all for coming. As you are aware this special meeting of the Accreditation Board was requested by the Governor, responding to numerous allegations of impropriety involving administration and faculty."

There was an unsettling movement of numerous chairs as the audience expressed their opinions without vocal response. All except one, who lowered his head as if to sneeze and barked, "Bullshit."

"Please," Ramblewood implored, "we ask you to withhold any comments and offer us the opportunity to conduct this meeting in an orderly fashion." He offered a dramatic pause before continuing. "First, if there are any students in attendance, we must ask you to leave the premises." He once again raised his hand to his brow and surveyed the audience. "Good. This hearing is only open to college administration, faculty, and other interested parties that received notice. I also ask that all recording devises be disabled and that all cell phones be

3

shut off." Another pause as numerous electronic messages announced terminated cell phone connections.

"Good. I believe we can begin. It is important to note, this is merely a preliminary investigatory hearing, allowing both administrators and faculty to express their view and opinions regarding the allegations. Serious as they are, there may be reasonable explanations, and that's what this hearing is all about; finding out the truth, no matter where it leads us. We must remember, the most important mission we have is to promote excellence in education and maintain an image of intellectual and moral competence. I am sure we can all agree on that."

There were mumurs and a few affirmative shakes of heads and one, "What an asshole," comment, just loud enough to generate a chuckle.

Ramblewood glanced at both his peers at the table and shook his head in disgust. Then he looked down at his yellow legal pad with scribbled notes and said, "Our first item is an allegation of faculty impropriety......... This involves, let's see," he reviewed his notes, "a phony, I believe." He looked at Dr. Burpee. "Is this correct Winnie? Do we have someone impersonating faculty?"

Winslow Burpee adjusted his glasses and sat up a little. He consulted his own legal pad before beginning. "I believe you may have a misprint, or perhaps you misread the allegation."

Ramblewood consulted his notes more closely. "Oh, it's a pony. Is that correct, a small horse?" He once again consulted his notes, adjusting his reading glasses and then with controlled concern in his voice asked, "We're talking about a horse, in the science lab?"

"Yes, I believe that is what the allegation purports. The unauthorized use of an Equis Caballus Var carcus, or commonly known as a dead pony, for experiments of unknown characteristics in the science lab. The allegation further indicts William Robert Redbone as the faculty member present and involved in whatever took place." Burpee leaned back, obviously satisfied with his presentation of the facts.

The room fell silent.

Dr. Busch squirmed in her seat and attempted to pass gas. Dr. Burpee took his glasses off and feigned cleaning the lenses while he waited for further action. Ramblewood leaned back and looked at the ceiling, trying to gather his thoughts and control his moderate temperament.

Finally, Ramblewood leaned forward and with his mouth almost absorbing the microphone said in a low intimidating drawl, "Is Professor Redbone present?"

CHAPTER 1

The closing of the Super Value at the end of Main Street was bitter sweet in some respects. When the Wal-Mart opened at the other end of the same street, the town kind of tilted that way and traffic coasted to the mega-store with its fancy slogans and seemingly endless sales. Jim Scales, the general manager of the Super Value held on for a while, slicing margins and laying off staff, but it was all for naught. The owner of the small chain, Ralph Roush, with corporate offices in Cougar Falls knew the hole card was never going to turn in his favor, so he closed the store in a decisive manner.

On a dreary Monday morning, about six AM, the usual time Rowena Ringwald arrived at the store to begin the process of turning the lights on and unlocking all of the inner doors, opening the safe and funding the cash drawers, she found the store completely empty, with exception of a few broken containers of cottage cheese and one box of Frosty Flakes littering the vast expanse of cement floor. The shelves were gone. The signs highlighting items contained in each isle were gone. The coolers once stacked full of soda and beer were gone. Everything was gone.

Rowena stood in the doorway, holding her keys, her mouth agape, wanting to scream or something, but nothing came across her vocal cords.

Finally, she pulled out her cell phone and dialed the Sheriff's office.

"Hinkley County Sheriff, what's your emergency?" Marge Stoffer had just put the coffee on, her dispatcher shift starting at six as well, and was about to sit down and review the call log from the night before when the phone rang.

"Marge, this is Rowena. I'm at the store, and, and, it's gone. The whole store is gone. Someone stole the whole store. I mean, the building is still here, but everything else is gone.…. The safe, I wonder if they got in the safe?" Rowena rushed through the door toward the area that once housed the office.

Marge yelled into the phone, "Rowena stop. Hold your horses, nobody stole nothin'."

But Rowena wasn't listening. She charged through what once was the customer service counter and flung open the unlocked office door and found it completely empty. Not even a pencil or piece of paper. A large hole in the wall left little doubt that the safe was gone too.

"Marge, they took everything. That safe had to weigh a thousand pounds."

"Rowena, slow down and listen, nobody stole nothin'. Mr. Roush, you know, the owner, he sent a crew in last night and they cleaned the place out. He called us but made it clear he didn't want the store closing to be made public. I'm sorry Rowena. Hey, I heard Ed's looking for a night manager at the Kountry Kitchen."

7

Rowena still held the phone to her ear but wasn't listening after she heard the part about cleaning the place out. She whispered, staring at the empty room, "That dirty rotten bastard. I've spent twenty two years cleaning up spills and…., and listening to peoples complaints about rotten bananas and he ain't even got the gonies to tell me I'm done."

"Rowena, you still there?"

Rowena continued her monotonous tone, talking to the phone, but really talking to herself. "People are going to start showing up for work, and there ain't nothing here. There ain't no groceries, there ain't no jobs, just an empty piece of shit building. What am I supposed to tell them? Oh, you'll find another job. Yeah, go down to the drug store; oh wait a minute, that closed last month too."

"Rowena, you alright? You want me to call Jerry and have him come down? You know, console you or something. I mean, maybe he can help you talk to the other employees."

She caught the last part about her husband and said, "What? Call Jerry? Are you kidding? He finds out about this, he may go over to Cougar Falls, to Roush's house, and kick that little bastard's ass, that's assuming some other employee, or ex-employee hasn't already done it." She thought for a minute. "I wonder if Jim knew about this all along. Did Scales call you about this?"

Marge hesitated too long trying to skirt the question about Jim Scales, the store's general manager.

"Got to go Marge," she said decisively, disconnecting the phone and walking through the empty store to the front entrance. She turned and took one more look before stepping outside.

The movers left a wood block near the door; an eight by eight oily piece of oak they apparently discarded in their rush. Rowena looked at it and without hesitation, picked it up and with all the strength her small torso could muster, flung it through the big window that had Super Value painted in multi-color script. The loud crash sent shivers down her back and drew the first, and probably the last smile of the long day.

*

Jim Scales lived at the other end of town on a tree lined street with a white picket fence surrounding the well manicured yard. The twice weekly Hinkley Messenger still lay on the front porch and there were no discernible lights on in the house.

Rowena parked on the street and marched up the sidewalk to the front door, picking up the newspaper on the way. She gave three stout whacks using the large clapper hanging on the giant red front door.

At first nothing stirred, and then she could hear footsteps approaching the door.

The door swung in and Scales stood in front of her, bathrobe open and wrinkled striped pajamas protruding. They both stared at each other, Rowena's face so red, the blue veins pulsing in her forehead looked like a roadmap.

"Rowena, I didn't expect you so early."

"You're lucky I don't carry a gun." She threw the paper at his chest and it bounced off landing at his feet."

Scales took a half step back. "Now don't go all blurry on me, Rowena. You knew this was coming, it was just a matter of time."

"*Time*, how much time is twenty two years?" Tears started to well and she grew louder with each syllable. "Twenty two years of carrying your bags... Yes Jim... Sure Jim, I'll do that... Sure Jim, I'll work extra so you can go golf... Sure Jim, I'll clean the toilets because Mr. Roush, that rotten bastard, is coming so you two can go to the country club for lunch."

"Now Rowena," Scales looked over his shoulder wondering if his wife was going to offer backup, "I did everything I could, for as long as I could, but it was inevitable. Wal-Mart was kicking our butt."

Rowena wiped the streaming tears from her eyes with her sleeve and drew a step closer, straining to get up in Scales face. "You don't get it do you? This isn't about *Wal-Mart*. This isn't about some wipe-ass job. This is about you and me. This is about thinking you have a friend. This is about a small town that sticks together, that don't scheme and wiggle and lie..... You told me last week, don't worry, the store's holding its own, your job's good. *Didn't you?*"

"Well yeah, but I just found out Saturday. I'm not kidding Rowena. Roush didn't even call me. He had the regional guy call me and tell me the store was closing and that the trucks would be there Sunday, and they'd take my pension if I told anyone."

Rowena held her stare, trying to decipher the truth from fiction.

"I mean, I knew the store was going to close. Everybody knew that...... Well not everybody." Scales looked over his shoulder again. "You want to come in, have some coffee."

"You bet your ass, not everybody knew. Did Billy Bob Redbone know?" Billy Bob ran the meat department.

"Well, I guess not."

"Did Doris know?" Doris was head checkout cashier.

"Well, probably not….. But Rowena."

"Don't but me, Jim. Nobody knew because you hid it. Just like that sleazy bastard that owns the place."

Scales exhaled and rubbed his forehead. "I don't mean it was announced or anything. I mean the writing was on the wall. Everyone could see it coming. You can't do half as much business and continue like nothing happened." Scales realized his robe was open and maybe other things were exposed as well, so he wrapped the robe and affixed the draw string. "Look Rowena, I'm sorry I couldn't be more forthcoming on this, but I've got something else I've been working on and I think you will be a perfect fit. I'm going to need an Executive Assistant, or better yet, maybe a Dean of Women. Like I said, I saw this coming, so I decided it was time for a career change."

"A what?" Rowena ran her sleeve across her eyes again and leaned against the porch railing like she was going to feint. The stress of the morning's events were catching up and overwhelming the meager amount of adrenalin left in her system.

Scales reached out and grasped her arm. "Come in and let's have a cup of coffee and I'll tell you all about what I've been working on.

CHAPTER 2

Scales led Rowena into the dining room where a big table, that sat at least eight, was covered with papers, binders, and all sorts of official looking government forms.

His wife sauntered down the stairs, hair in curlers and blinders pulled up on her forehead like starlet sunglasses. She stopped with a jolt when she saw there was a guest.

"Rowena, what are you doing here? It's hardly daylight. Jim, why didn't you tell me we had company?" She patted her head, realizing she was still in curlers and had the mask on her head. "Oh, for goodness sake."

As she turned and rushed toward the stairs, Scales said, "Hon, can you make us some coffee?" He looked at Rowena, "Maybe after she gets dressed."

Rowena scanned the table, sighed, and said, "What's all this, job applications? Jim, I'm fifty four, barely graduated from high school, have experience making change in a defunct grocery store, and now you want me to start filling out job applications? I'd rather go to Ralphie's and drink until I puke. At least then I'd have a reason for puking. And right now, the way my guts feel, all of this end of the house could be in trouble."

"Just keep it together while I explain. And if you really need it, the downstairs bath is right next to the stairs. What you are looking at here is our future, The Hinkley Community College, LLC."

"What's an LLC? Sounds like some kind of sex toy you'd find at the strip club in Cougar Falls."

Scales gave Rowena a 'whatever' look and continued. "I've been working on this for about a year or more, ever since I started to get the vibes from Roush that he was considering closing the store. I knew he'd never promote me to the corporate office, I'm too old, and besides, his kid, the one that did 2 years for cocaine possession and has rings through everything on his body including his pecker, and don't ask me how I know that, doesn't like me.

"Anyway, I was at this meeting in Peoria, and they held it at the community college; nice place, kind of out away from the crummy downtown in the nice part where most of the more affluent people live. There were kids everywhere, carrying books, smoking pot, you know, doing kid stuff."

"Smoking pot, right out in the open?"

"I'm just blowing smoke up your skirt, Rowena. No, I mean it looked real, you know, educational. So, I start asking around. Is this a State school? How longs it been here, stuff like that. And, I find out it's privately owned, an accredited school, can charge tuition, get kids student loans, but it's for profit. I say, I didn't know schools could be run for profit. They say, sure they can, as long as you meet certain criteria and keep the board happy. I ask what board, and no one could give me that answer."

Rowena's eyes were growing heavy and Scales wife came out of the kitchen with two coffee mugs.

Janet Scales asked, "So, why so early Rowena, something wrong at the store?"

Rowena gave Scales a hard look. Janet took the bait and gave her husband the same blank stare.

"I suppose you didn't tell her either," Rowena said with a smirk.

"Tell me what?"

There was silence with exception of a garbage truck somewhere in the distance crashing cans into its hopper.

"Well, the store closed this weekend." Scales studied a blank paper in front of him.

"What store?" His wife asked, kind of nonchalant, taking a sip of coffee.

"The Super Value, what other store is there? Roush closed the store. Caput, closed, out of business, whatever you want to call it, it's not there anymore."

Janet put her hand over her mouth with bulging eyes. "But, but, where will I get my groceries?"

"For God's sake Janet, I, we don't have a job anymore, and you're worried about *groceries*? That's why Rowena's here. The store's closed. That's it. So, let's just get on with our lives."

Janet Scales burst into tears. "What are we going to do? What about the country club? What will they all say? You are unemployed. Oh my God, you're unemployed." She continued to sob and left the room.

Scales looked at Rowena with that *see what I have to live with* look.

"Anyway," he continued, "the more I looked at this college, a plan started to take hold. What's the one thing Hinkley doesn't have? Well, maybe not the only thing, but what's an important thing we don't have? A college, or at least some form of higher education, like a vocational school or something. I know there's the Institute of Higher Learning over in the Falls, but why should our kids have to drive thirty or forty miles to go to college, when they could get it right here?

"So, I started doing some research." He waved his hand across the table. "And do you know, there are government grants offering seed money to start a school? I mean real money, Rowena. Hundreds of thousands of dollars, just sitting there waiting for someone to send in the application. And guess who sent the application in? You betcha, *me*. And guess who got the grant? Right again, *me*, or should I say, Hinkley Community College, LLC." He rifled through a stack of papers and pulled out an official looking letter. "Look at this. It's from the Illinois Department of Commerce, Re-education and Re-training Department. They say they are giving Hinkley Community College, LLC an interest free loan of $338,475.85 to be funded the first of next month. I'm not sure where the eighty five cents came from, but I'll take it."

Rowena belched and rubbed her mouth with her sleeve. She started to get up. "Good for you, Jim. That should pay your country club dues, for what, the next three years. Meanwhile, the rest of us will be standing at the food bank waiting for the turnip wagon to show up." She turned to leave.

15

"Wait Rowena, don't you get it? This is an opportunity. Not only for me, but for you, and, I don't know, Billy Bob, and Roy; we'll need a janitor. That's what Roy did at the store. He can do it at the college. Billy Bob ran the meat department; he knows anatomy, probably better than most of the doctors around here, he can teach science. John did maintenance on the refrigeration, he can teach the HVAC class. We'll get a mechanic from Fred's Fords to teach the auto shop class. You starting to get the idea?"

"Yeah, sure, and what will I teach, how to run a cash register and clean toilets?"

"Look Rowena, you're missing the point. What's really lacking in education today? It's real life experience. If you wanted your kid to learn fire safety, would you rather he learn from a fireman with ten years real fire fighting experience, or some kid fresh out of university with a degree in camp fire management. That's what our schools are missing, teachers with real life experience. Yeah, if I wanted my kid to learn about running and managing a business, you would be the one I would want teaching the class."

Rowena sighed, still not convinced and took a sip of coffee, hoping to settle her stomach. "Where you gonna put this, this college, or whatever?"

"Ah, glad you asked. I kind of went behind Roush's back and called his real estate guy, anonymously of course, as an agent for Hinkley Community College LLC, and inquired about any buildings in the Hinkley area that might be for rent in the near future. Sure enough, he said he couldn't give me the address but he was sure there was a building that would be available. I thought he was going to pee himself, he was so anxious to get me to sign a lease. They've closed three stores in the last six months, so they are sitting on a bunch of vacant buildings. Anyway, he said Roush Holdings would be willing to offer three months free rent in exchange for a three year lease. Anyway, I know I'm getting too technical here, but, bottom line is, we can be in the store remodeling starting next week and be ready for fall enrollment this year." Scales leaned back in his chair, satisfied that he had convinced Rowena the plan was failsafe.

She stared at the blank wall. "Twenty two years, and for what? I don't even have a pension to speak of. Put some money in their 401K plan, but that all went down the tubes in the recession, all except what the pension guy took. He still belongs to the country club and drives a Cadillac."

"Look Rowena, I'm sure this all seems a little overwhelming, but, stick with me on this, okay?"

Rowena turned her blank stare to Scales and without the slightest inflection said, "I'm going home." She pushed herself back from the table, rose and walked toward the front door. She heard a sob and noticed Janet Scales sitting in the dark living room, her head in her hands, talking to herself, something about the country club.

CHAPTER 3

The HINKLEY MESSENGER

Saturday Edition

Headline: *COMMUNITY COLLEGE RIBBON CUTTING*

The Hinkley Community College is now officially accepting candidates for enrollment. The honorable Dr. James Scales officiated the ceremony Thursday evening at the former Super Value store, now remodeled to accommodate what Dr. Scales referred to as the Hinkley Center for Higher Learning. Helping cut the ribbon were Chet Sadinski, County Commissioner, Harold Hanover, President of the Hinkley Chamber of Commerce and Jerry Smithy, Superintendent of the Hinkley County school system. Following the ribbon cutting ceremony, Dr. Scales led a tour of the primary campus that includes four separate classroom laboratories surrounding a central auditorium and student lounge that includes a large vending machine selection, soon to be replaced by a full commercial kitchen, explained Dr. Scales, to enhance the skills of those enrolled in the Restaurant Management Certificate of Accomplishment Degree Program.

In addition to the Restaurant Management program, the college offers Certificate of Accomplishment degrees in Elderly and Invalid Care, Heating and Air Conditioner Repair, Automobile Maintenance and Repair, and what Dr. Scales proudly called and spelled out, the Dollars and Sense of Business Management degree. Each program is taught by a professional with years of experience in the specific field of interest, Dr. Scales said. He went on to expound upon the mission of the school, primarily to bring real life experience to the classroom by employing professionals in each field of endeavor.

Dr. James Scales, primary investor in the private, for profit school, was the former General Manager of the Super Value Grocery Store, prior to its closing last March. When asked where he achieved his doctorate degree, and in what field of endeavor, he responded that the degree was honorary and would not offer further details. The limited biographical data available to the Messenger indicates Dr. Scales managed a Sunoco gas station prior to taking the position of Assistant Manager of the Super Value in Hinkley. He graduated from Cougar Falls High School. He is past President of the Hinkley Kiwanis Club and is currently serving as Committee Chair of the Dining and Entertainment Committee at the Hinkley Country Club.

Enrollment for the fall semester is currently underway. Students can enroll on line at hinkleylearning center.com or by calling the school enrollment office during regular business hours. Credit cards are accepted and counselors are available to assist in preparation of applications for low interest student loans.

The HINKLEY MESSENGER
Saturday Edition
Classified Ad: Help Wanted

The Hinkley Community College is seeking an experienced person to act in its behalf in the recruitment of entrance level applicants for higher education. Prior sales experience helpful but not necessary. Lucrative commissions paid on a bi-weekly basis including benefits and bonuses based on production. Travel required within a 100 mile radius of operation. Immediate opening. Send resume to hinkleylearningcenter.com or call 1-800-Hinkley for an interview appointment.

Rowena sat behind her desk, clear with exception of a ball point pen holder, a small desk calendar from her insurance agent and a picture of her daughter in a graduation gown standing in front of her house. A picture of a bald eagle perched on a tree snag hung on the wall behind her. Two other chairs sat on either side of the office door, one vacant and the other occupied by Billy Bob Redbone, his arms crossed on his chest, dressed in blue jeans, a denim shirt with sweat stains under each arm and dirty cowboy boots, crossed on his outstretched legs.

"Where's your hat?" Rowena said with a hint of distaste. "You're gonna come in here dressed like a bum, you might as well finish the picture with a dirty cowboy hat."

"It ain't like I got to impress nobody, do I?" There ain't no students yet." Redbone slouched even further into the chair.

"Billy Bob, you're gonna get fired before you ever start. And dress up your talk a little too. Ain't ain't a word. About the time you start trying to teach these kids how to cut meat, or whatever you are supposed to do, and they realize you can't even speak English, at least proper English, they're gonna want their money back."

"How many kids we got so far?" Billy Bob pulled a pouch of Redman chew from his back pocket.

"Oh no, you're not eatin' that stuff in here. Next thing, you'll be lookin' for someplace to spit. Just put it away..... So far, we got eight students. You hear that, they're called students, not kids."

"Rowena, I've know'd you for what, twenty some years, and now you want to go and get all high fallutin' on me. Come on, it ain't...., isn't gonna happen. You know the old sayin', you can take 'em off the farm, but you can't take 'em out of the farm." Redbone looked at the ceiling. "It's something like that. You know what I mean."

Rowena shook her head and smiled. "You're right about one thing, you sure aren't going to change."

*

The store had one second story balcony office that was equipped with a two way mirror so Scales, when he ran the grocery store, could watch for shop lifters along with his other management responsibilities. In his new position as President of the college, he again occupied the upper office, now re-furnished with a large cherry veneer desk and matching credenza, leather reclining executive chair with duel matching overstuffed chairs in front. The office was arranged with the two way mirror behind the credenza, so when Scales swirled around in his chair, he looked out over the auditorium. This gave him great pleasure, imagining the room bustling with students, each representing a large tuition.

In the corner of the office stood a large easel, with numerous advertising brochures depicting the many educational tools available at the college. Scales enlisted the help of an advertising agency in Cougar Falls to create the new image and subsequently mailed a brochure and enrollment application to every high school graduate within a one hundred mile radius. The resulting return on investment was not encouraging so he was looking forward to his next appointment, an interview with a prospective recruiter.

Randall Elliot Lupinski, after stopping three times for directions because his GPS map had no recognition of Hinkley Community College, pulled into the parking lot a few minutes late for his scheduled interview. The first thing he saw was a wind ravaged canvas sign draped over the old Super Value sign, identifying Hinkley Community College. The first impression was further depressed by a section of plate glass in the front of the building that was covered with plywood. The balance of the building still had the appearance of a vacant grocery store.

His perception was further marred when he walked through the front door of the school into the auditorium, which was void of any activity and somewhat bland to the eye, and heard nothing but the echo of his own footsteps. He had expected much more based on the ad posted in the *Educator's Employment Weekly,* given the ad depicted great financial opportunity with a well established institution.

Billy Bob Redbone sauntered out of Rowena's office on his way to lunch at Ralphie's bar and confronted Lupinski. "Help ya?"

Lupinski wore a Ralph Lauren blue blazer, light pink button down shirt, Harvard striped tie and khaki pants. His tassel loafers were void of any dust and appeared to be spit shined. "I'm here to see Dr. Scales, can you direct me to the administrative office building? I've obviously been misdirected."

Billy Bob gave Lupinski the once over and said, "Yeah, I'd say you been misdirected alright." He turned toward Rowena's office and yelled, "Rowena, there's a dude out here wants to see the Doc', he in?"

Rowena scurried out of her office, straightening her skirt and pulling at her blouse, showing a big smile as she pushed Billy Bob out of the way. "Why yes, I believe Dr. Scales is expecting you." She again pushed Billy Bob further toward the door. "I'll show you to his office."

Billy Bob turned and headed toward the door. "I could'a done that, had I know'd that's all he wanted."

23

"Don't mind him," Rowena said, looping her arm around Lupinski's jacketed elbow, "it's his day off, so he's kind of casual. He's our science professor. You know how they can be, kind of peculiar, too smart for their own good sometimes."

Lupinski looked over his shoulder through the windows into the parking lot, making sure Redbone wasn't near his car. "What kind of science, what's he teach?"

Rowena didn't have any idea, she had just heard Scales say Redbone was going to teach some kind of science. "Anatomy, primarily, he's very experienced in areas of dissection, but there may be other classes too."

She led him up the stairs to Scales office, the door still displaying the *Employees Only* banner from the grocery store.

After Rowena gave a slight knock, Scales opened the door and said, "Come in, come in, have a seat. You must be Mr. Lupinski, I've been expecting you. Thank you Rowena." He gave her a small nudge back out the door and closed it in her face. "I'm Dr. Scales, but, Rowena must have already told you that. We spoke when you called. Well, what do you think of our little school? It's coming along, you know. It takes time, but we're proud of it, so far." Scales threw his arm up in an arching motion in front of the two way mirror. "This is our student activity center and auditorium. Of course, classes are not in session now, but, next month, this will be our hub of activity."

Lupinski sat, somewhat stunned by what he had observed so far. "Uh, is this the only building?"

"Well, yes, so far. So, tell me about Randy Lupinski." Scales sat back in his leather executive chair, elbow on the arm rest, chin wedged between his thumb and finger and smiled.

24

"It's Randall, Randall Lupinski, and there's not that much to tell. I graduated eighth in my class from Marquette, Bachelor of Science Business School with a minor in psychology. Did my graduate studies at Notre Dame, off campus at a satellite but haven't finished that yet. Still have my thesis to complete. I've been working as a teaching fellow at a small school, but want to put my business training into practice, so I have been interviewing."

"Ready to go after the big bucks, huh? Well, you may have stumbled into a gold mine, my friend." Scales pulled open a lower desk drawer and took out a fat folder and lay it on the desk. "I've done a little research that you may be interested in, that is, if you want to take this to the next level, *Randall*." He pulled out the top paper and handed it to Lupinski.

"This data, start at the top there *Randall*, shows the number of adults age eighteen and above that graduated from high school this year within a one hundred mile radius of our school. That pie chart, you're familiar with pie charts aren't you, eighth in your class *Randall*, shows the percentage that went on to some form of higher education. Pretty low percentage, isn't it *Randall?*

"Now Randy, sorry, *Randall*," Scales pulled another paper out and lay it in front of Lupinski, "this shows the average income of those kids families. I know, driving here from wherever, you thought you were out in the sticks, but this is farm country, and you may think that guy in the old pickup truck is a poor farmer, but think again. And, he would like nothing better than to have his ignorant kid that barely made it through industrial arts class in high school attend an institution

25

of higher learning and get some sort of certificate or diploma. That's where we come in. We don't have to recruit the kids, we have to recruit the parents. Hell, the kids would just assume stay at home and bale hay or slop the hogs. It's the parents that need the shove. Know what I mean, *Randall?*"

Lupinski's shoulders sank an inch each time Scales gave him the Randall tag. All of his basic instincts told him to stand up and walk out of the office without so much as a wave goodbye. But, and it was a big but, his checking account was on empty, his so called teaching fellow job was gratis in exchange for online graduate classes, and his father had cut his allowance as stimulus to find a job. He had pretty much run out of options, short of moving home. So, he did the only thing he could, suck it up and hope he could negotiate some sort of advance along with getting the job.

Lupinski looked up from the paper and said, "Very impressive Dr. Scales. Is your Doctorate in actuarial science?"

"Something like that," Scales replied smiling. "I take it, after seeing my research, you may be interested in becoming our Director of Admissions and Financial Aid."

"Well, I've had several offers, and this seems to be an entry level position...."

"Cut the crap *Randall.* And by the way, they may call you *Randall* at Notre Dame, but if you work here, you're Randy." Scales pulled a three ring binder from the drawer and lay it on the desk. "This, Randy, is your bible. Assuming you decide to take this entry level position, you will need to memorize these scripts. I got this system from a friend that works at another school, and by the way, he told me he made six figures in

26

commissions last year… Make this entry level position sound a little more appealing, Randy? In that binder you'll find a complete sales guide, from the initial call, to the final ask, it's all there. There isn't an objection that isn't covered. Like, my kids not smart enough…. We have tutors…. My kid wets the bed…. We have plastic seat covers, and on and on.

Lupinski peeled page after page, scanning the information. "This sounds more like a used car sales position than a school admissions director. I've never sold anything. I don't know."

"Playing hard to get, huh. Okay, how does this sound, our annual tuition starts at around five thousand, depending on how many hours the kid takes, but full time will get it up around that. Every kid you sign up, you get ten percent of the first year's tuition, that's five hundred Randy, in case they didn't teach math at Marquette. Now let's say, conservatively, in the next month and a half, prior to when the fall semester starts, you sign up thirty kids. That's about one a day." Scales held his hand out like he was holding a calculator and tapped with his finger. "Let's see, that's fifteen grand, Randy, and you didn't have to invest a dime, just dress in those fine duds you got on and make a few house calls. Before you know it, I'll probably be asking you for a loan."

Lupinski continued to scan page after page but wasn't reading a word. Fifteen thousand kept resonating in his head. A new BMW flashed before his eyes. Weekends spent on Michigan Avenue in downtown Chicago seemed within reach, and all he had to do was sell a few…. A few what? That was the thing that was sticking in the sprocket of his churning brain. What would he be selling, an education, in this place?

"Earth to Randy, you still with us?"

"Uh, just scanning this booklet. Okay, how many students does the school have now, or enrolled for the fall?" He looked up and caught a twitch in Scales fake smile.

"Well, we are just getting started you know. We just received our certification about three weeks ago, just starting to get the wheels rolling, so to speak. That's why it's so important to get someone in this position pronto. So, what do you think?"

Lupinski held his stare as Scales bluff smile started to fade. "How many?"

"Eight, but we haven't really rolled out the red carpet yet. I mean, once we get the call center setting up appointments, we shouldn't have any problem getting at least a hundred students enrolled in the next month."

Lupinski rubbed his forehead. "That's it, eight? And what's this call center you are talking about?"

"That's all set up already. We are using a call center that originates, well, I'm not sure where it originates, but, I gave them a list of eight hundred names and when I give them the word, they start calling and setting up appointments. You should have no trouble getting ten solid leads a week. Sell, I mean, enroll five of those and you made twenty five hundred bucks." Scales stood up. It was time to close the deal. "Come on, I'll show you your new office."

Scales led Lupinski out into the hall and down the stairs. "Need to have you on the first floor, in case you're dealing with a cripple, know what I mean."

"You mean someone that's disabled?"

"Yeah, that's what I meant, disabled. See, that's why I need you; you know that kind of stuff. Hey, there might even be some free government money if we get some *disabled* kids, you think?" Scales opened a door, and a musty, spoiled vegetable smell met them. "Haven't got this cleaned up quite yet, so, you'll have to use your imagination, but, I'll get you some furniture, paint this up so it's clean. Oh yeah, be sure you bring your diplomas and stuff to hang on the wall. That's going to be real important; impressive to some kid and his parents, thinking there's a diploma in the future to hang on the fireplace." Scales flipped on the wall light switch and the room came into focus and the smell became even more pungent.

"What's that smell?" Lupinski tried to hold his breath. The back wall was uncovered concrete block, apparently the outside wall of the building. The inner patrician walls appeared to be drywall, with stains and graffiti everywhere. The concrete floor seemed to be the origin of the smell, with a myriad of dried spills of unknown, rotting, organic material.

"This is where we, they, stored returned items when this was a grocery store. The smell kind of got absorbed into the walls, I guess. A little paint and you'll never even notice it. Besides, most of your work will be in the homes of these kids, with the parents. Remember, it's the parents you have to sell, and since we're not a state school, they will have to co-sign tuition notes." Scales yanked Lupinski's arm, pulling him away from the door and slammed it shut. "Let's go out into the student center and we'll nail this down."

Lupinski sniffed at his coat sleeve wondering if any stench had clung to him. As they passed the front entrance he once again glanced to make sure his car hadn't been stolen by the so called science teacher and followed Scales into the large, mostly vacant, center area of the former grocery store. The cement floor remained unpainted and showed unstained areas where shelves had once held merchandise. The balance showed well worn cart paths and deeply imbedded stains. There were a few metal folding chairs scattered around showing no semblance of order.

Scales pulled two chairs together and sat down, pointing without comment at the other chair directing Lupinski to do the same. "So, you're up to speed, when do you want to start, and before you answer, if it's anything beyond forty eight hours from now, enough time for you to drive to wherever you came from, say goodbye, and drive back, it won't do." He crossed his arms and sat back.

Lupinski scratched his chin, and for the first time, felt motivated to ask some serious questions and express an opinion. "No offense, Dr. Scales," he turned his head and scanned the surroundings, "this looks like it could be a hard sell. I just don't see parents wanting to send their kid to a converted grocery store to get educated. And then, I'm not sure what the education is. Are we talking vocational school? Are we talking college prep? Who is going to do the teaching? I met, or ran into, the science teacher, what's his qualifications?"

Scales shook his head. "Randy, Randy, Randy..., I guess I had you pegged all wrong. It's probably all that uppity education. I mean, I thought you looked pretty down to earth, but maybe not. Well, let's just forget this, okay? You go on back to the big city and let us country folk go on about our business."

Lupinski had a flash of his BMW being towed back to the showroom. "Wait, I'm just asking some questions, trying to get a feel, you know, of what your dream is, the mission so to speak; what you want this place to be."

"Well Randy, let me lay it out for you. Folks around here don't judge a book by its cover. You get where I'm coming from. Now, you take Ralphie's, down the street yonder. You probably wouldn't step in there because there's nothing on the menu over five bucks and some of the seats have tears in the upholstery. But people around here think its fine dining and a Saturday night at Ralphie's, well, to most, it's quite an occasion. Folks 'd rather go to Hanover's hardware and pay five dollars more for a shovel than go to Wal-Mart, just because they get to talk to Harold and know that that five dollars will probably get turned around and end up back in somebody else's pocket locally, not in China or India.

"So, when those parents come in here and look around, they're not looking for fancy decorations or expensive tax dollar funded movie theaters and student lounges. They're looking for local people that are going to teach their kids how to get a job, a real job, not some social worker job the government pays for. And that's what we have for them, real people that came from real jobs with real life experience, something I doubt you've had much of."

Randy took the brow beating in an adult manner, holding his head up and keeping eye contact, but he couldn't help thinking, *what have I gotten myself into*. The night before he had eaten Chicago pizza washed down with artisan beer in a swank, retro, micro brewery on the west end of Michigan Avenue. Now he

31

sat in a vacant grocery store, being dressed down by a quasi con artist, on the verge of taking a job selling diplomas. Not exactly what the President of his class at Marquette spoke of at graduation when he described, "Bettering our cultural environment through application of our enhanced learning experience." Of course, he already had a six figure job lined up with a national commodity brokerage house in Chicago, bettering his own cultural environment, probably with one hundred dollar bills.

"Well Randy, what's it gonna be. Shall I have appointments scheduled for you starting Monday? I can have that office ready to hang those diplomas." Scales smiled broadly and held out his hand to shake on the deal.

Randy almost choked out his next sentence. "I'll need a five hundred dollar advance."

Scales smile was swiped from his face faster than a loose one hundred dollar bill on a New York City sidewalk. He leaned forward, his hand on one knee for support. "A what?"

Randy tried for some composure but his voice cracked. "Look, things are a little tight right now. And, well, you are asking me to travel all over God's half acre chasing these kids. That costs money, gas money, mileage on my car, stuff like that."

"Do I have stupid written on my forehead? Or maybe there's a 'kick me' sign pinned to the back of my shirt. You really think I'm gonna give you five hundred dollars on the hope you are going to show up Monday morning?" Scales shook his head, chuckled and leaned back.

"Well, no, I don't expect you to give me the money right now. Well, maybe not all of it. See, I've got to drive back home, get things straight, pack, and I'm just a little short. Actually, I need some gas to get back." There, he said it. He was broke; couldn't even buy a hambuger, if they have a MacDonalds, he wasn't sure.

Scales studied his expression, looking for a hint of cunning and didn't see it. "Okay," he said sighing, "here's what I'm going to do. Rowena's gonna ride with you down to the Speedy Fill-up, get you enough gas to get home, and maybe a Coke. Then, assuming you can scrape together enough change out of the couch, you are going to show up here Monday ready to start enrolling students. If you have to sleep in your office, we'll get you a cot, whatever it takes. I need one hundred smiling faces walking through that door by the first day of classes, and you my friend, are going to make that happen. Deal?" He once again extended the hand of contractual obligation.

Randy sheepishly responded by shaking the hand and forcing a smile and choked out, "Deal."

CHAPTER 4

Marla Todd lay on her unmade bed, holding a mirror with one hand and tweezers with the other, examining a festering spot on her latest tattoo, an iron cross scrunched between her breasts with the ends of the cross bar morphing into fingers that pointed at each nipple. There were substantial bruises as well resulting from the artist squeezing, pinching and squashing in an attempt to provide a taught surface for his needle, at least that was his excuse. She had not suffered any irregular hemorrhaging or infection from the fourteen prior adventures into body painting, as the artists called it, so she envisioned marching back to Tattoos Are Us, located next to Adult Toys and Videos Are Us, in Cougar Falls and demanding her money back. It was just a thought; maybe after she went out to the garage and smoked a joint; *or*, maybe not.

Marla graduated from Hinkley High, but only after her father petitioned the school principal, a personal friend and bowling partner on the Knights of Columbus bowling team, to correct her final grade report, replacing the failing grade in Senior Choir to a D, bringing her grade point average to a 1.0, the minimum necessary to receive a diploma.

So far, her less than gratifying exit from high school had been followed by one arrest for possession of alcohol by a minor, two violations for driving under suspension, well, actually three, but the one stop by Sheriff Deputy Smiling Dog Santini was excused after a quick romp in the back seat of the cruiser. After the second violation, the magistrate had advised any further indiscretions could result in actual incarceration, so, desperate times require desperate measures. And besides, Santini was well known as an advocate for dispensing his own justice in lieu of wasting the court's time.

Marla spent most days since exiting the hallowed halls of Hinkley High sleeping off the perils of alcohol and marijuana abuse from the night before. She timed her daily departure from home to correspond with her father's return from his eight hour shift as assistant manager of maintenance at the Olatagwa Casino. Her mother, a part time cashier at the Super Value, now unemployed, sat on the back porch most of the day chain smoking and discussing on the phone the family's financial dilemma with whatever unemployed relative or family friend would listen.

Marla walked through the galley kitchen, searching and finding a stale Twinkie wedged between a package of moldy bread and a can of baked beans. She fished a coke from the refrigerator and turned to head out the front door, distancing herself from her mother. The last thing she needed, considering the pounding headache that was reminding her of why she should never again drink tequila, was another diatribe from her mother about the evils of alcohol and the fact that she was starting to look a lot like a female version of Dennis Rodman, only much shorter. That, plus the fact she had on a halter top that barely covered her chest, clipped short shorts that barely covered her crotch, and enough eye liner to make Elizabeth Taylor jealous. All this, combined with enough piercings to make her body look like one giant key ring, led to numerous out of control shouting matches.

As she stepped from the kitchen, she overheard a disturbing bit of her mother's phone conversation. Something about Marla and college, and even more frightening, it sounded like she was serious. There was no laugh, like, yeah, as if that would ever happen, or, on a cold day in hell. It sounded like she was bragging about it.

Marla inched closer to the patio door.

"Yeah, Jim Scales called me personally. After I called him every name in the book; and I mean every name, for shutting down the store, he started telling me about the Community College. .... Yeah, I saw it in the paper too, but, you know, stuff like that's for the rich kids. Anyway, he tells me he can get Marla in and it won't cost that much, and then the government pays most of it.......... That's what I thought too, I mean, I don't particularly like you calling her stupid, I mean, they said she has a mild learning disability, anyway, he said grades don't matter, as long as she made it through high school, she can get enrolled........... Of course she'll do it. Marla's a good girl, just a little mixed up. It's that asshole boyfriend of her's, he's the one makes her do all that stuff."

Marla rubbed her temples trying to clear her head enough to digest what she was hearing. *She really thinks I'm going to go back to school? Like, get real!*

"What? You think Danny could get in? And you call Marla stupid, he couldn't spell cat if it was written on his shirt…….. You started it…….. Oh yeah……… Hello…… Hello.

Marla thought, *might as well get this over with right now.* She walked out to the patio, her mother sitting in a lounge chair, cigarette dangling from her lips, the phone still in her hand, preparing to dial another number.

"Hey mom."

Ruth Todd looked up, gave Marla's skimpy outfit the once over, shook her head in disgust, and continued dialing another number.

Marla tried to be cordial. "Who you callin'?"

Ruth stopped her number punching and looked back up. "Do you think you could get those shorts any smaller? What's the use of wearing them, they don't cover nothing." The cigarette smoke trailed up her face into her frizzed hair. "And what's that thing between your tits? It looks like crayon scribbles with a boil in the middle."

"Nice to see you too," Marla said sarcastically. "Uh, I thought I heard you talking about some sort of school or something. What's that all about?"

Ruth pulled a heavy drag on her cigarette and then stubbed it out in the overflowing ashtray on a stand next to the chair. "You're gonna go to college. Hopefully, they have some sort of girl's finishing class, teach you how to dress in public. You know, I promised you grandma you would make something of yourself, other than a walking inkpad."

37

"*What?*"

"Yeah, I set up the appointment for tonight at six o'clock. Your father will be home, *and so will you,* if you know what's good for you." She pulled another cigarette from the pack, plucked it in her mouth and lit it, all in one sweeping motion, like a good golf swing.

"Whoa, hold on a minute. I'm not going back to school. Like, I just got through with that nonsense, dealing with those idiots; I'm not doing it again. I'm eighteen; you can't make me do that. Like, there's a law against that or something, I think."

Ruth smirked, "So what, you're gonna spend the next part of your life sleeping until noon, drinking and smoking pot, all the while, living in this house? I don't think so, sister. And don't tell me you will move out. Where you gonna go? It sure isn't with that worthless piece of crap boyfriend. He couldn't find two pennies to rub together, and if he did, he isn't smart enough to do the rubbing."

"He's not my," Marla held up her hands making imaginary parentheses with her fingers and rolled her eyes, "*boyfriend.* He's just a friend."

"Just a friend, yeah, tell me he hasn't had his hand up those shorts. With friends like that, you're gonna end up in the gutter right beside them." Ruth blew smoke out of her nose with a snort.

Marla put her hand on her hip in an impressive belligerent stance. "Well, like, you can't make me go to school."

"Don't take that attitude with me, young lady. You may think you run things around here, but you don't. If I, we, your father and I, say you are going to college, then by God, you're going to college. Do you know how hard he works at the casino, just to feed and clothe you, and give you a home?"

Not this again, Marla thought. She had heard all of the rumors about her father and the cocktail waitresses, and for that matter, every other female employee in the casino. She even knew a couple of the younger girls he had hit on, and had a good laugh when they told her of his promises to teach them about sex, like he was some kind of stud. She knew where he stashed his Viagra and kept count, not wanting to inspire suspicion by taking too many, so she knew he wasn't having much success.

Maybe she should take a different tact, try to do the old switcheroo. "But what about my job?"

Ruth looked up, lips parted, cigarette hanging limp, speechless for a second. Then she slowly took the cigarette from her mouth and squinted a questioning gaze. *"What job?"*

"Well, like, I don't actually have it yet, but, Bud, down at the party shop, wants me to manage the place at night. Like, be the supervisor, or something. He's, like, interviewing, but, he said I was, well, his choice, probably." Marla looked at her wrist, like she was checking the time, even though she didn't where a watch. "Oops, got to go, have to check with Bud to see when I start. So, there's no reason to meet with the school people tonight. Thanks mom."

"Wait a minute." Ruth stubbed out another cigarette. "Hand me the phone book, it's next to the refrigerator."

"Who you calling?" Marla hesitated to fetch the phone book, anticipating the answer.

"Who you think? I'm calling Bud. I think you made that whole thing up. Vera, Bud's wife, she wouldn't let him hire

39

some young girl, especially after he got caught with his wiener in the wrong bun last year. So, we'll just give him a call."

"Like, I didn't say I had the job. I said, like, I applied. That's different."

Ruth lit another cigarette. "Kind of like, I didn't lie, I just told you half the truth, the half I wanted you to hear."

"Like, what time's he gonna be here?"

CHAPTER 5

Randy pulled into the driveway and parked behind a rusty pickup truck that was nosed up against a garage door that appeared not to have been used for quite some time. He surveyed the premises just to draw some reference as to what he might encounter at the door. The bungalow showed signs of neglect, but met the standards of the rest of the neighborhood. A cat slept on a swing suspended from the porch ceiling, with the serene scene complemented by some wilted flowers in a wooden planter next to the steps leading to the front door.

Scales gave him a file folder and the tab displayed Marla Todd as the potential student. Besides an enrollment application, alongside was one sheet of paper with a hand written bio on George and Ruth Todd; George, janitor at the casino and Ruth, unemployed. Their combined income estimated at $28,000, just above the poverty line; no mortgage on the house; no car loans; no other children; pre-qualified for a student loan of up to $15,000 per year.

Randy leaned back against the car head rest and took a deep breath. This was his first appointment; first attempt ever trying to sell anything; first time walking into the unknown. What if they have some kind of big, vicious dog? What if, what's his name, George comes to the door with a shotgun? What if they go for it? That's the big unknown.

He straightened his Harvard striped tie, stepped out of the car and headed for the front door. The cat looked up, yawned and resumed its slumber. He pressed the door bell button but there was no noticeable sound. He knocked on the wooden screen door and it rattled like it was going to fall off the hinges.

Marla came to the door, same casual dress from earlier in the day; same festering spot in between her breasts that had the magnetic effect of drawing one's attention to her adolescent bumps, whether you wanted to or not.

Marla greeted him, "Dude, you must be the guy from the school. Like, where did you get those clothes? You look like Jay Leno."

Randy stood motionless, and wordless. The amount of exposed skin along with the variety of piercings left him wondering what to do next. She was like a pop top experiment that went bad. He wanted to ask, *were you forced to do that*? Even worse, *did you pay someone to do that*?

"What's the matter dude, you never seen a tattoo before?"

"You must be Marla," he finally spit out.

"You must be the dude," Marla responded, "not like the Great Lebowski, more like the opposite kind of dude, the dude of the day." Marla laughed and when she opened her mouth, a small ring that was pierced through her tongue sparkled.

"Didn't that hurt?" Randy asked.

"What?"

42

"That thing that's stuck in your tongue."

"Naa, they put some junk on your tongue so you don't feel it." Marla looked over her shoulder and then stepped closer to Randy and looked him in the eye and whispered, "It makes my boyfriend go nuts."

From back in the house a gravelly voice yelled, "Marla, that the guy from the school? Bring him in the kitchen."

Randy followed Marla through the living room, equipped with a large flat screen TV and two recliners, into the kitchen where George and Ruth sat at each end of a vinyl clad table with chrome legs. Each had a cigarette dangling from their lips and a full ash tray on the table next to a cup of coffee. The stench from the cigarette smoke was only matched by the lingering odor of rancid grease. At first Randy thought there must be a yellow bug light in use but quickly realized it was the nicotine stained walls that gave off the amber cast.

"This here's Ruth and I'm George. I suppose you already met Marla. God damn Mar, put some clothes on. He ain't here for no porn show."

Marla slumped down in a chair opposite Randy and crossed her arms, pumping up her chest, exposing the inked fingers on her new tattoo. When she caught his eye, she slipped her tongue out just enough to show the silver ring.

George broke the silence. "As you can see, Marla ain't your normal kid, but don't let her fool you, she's smart as a whip. What she needs is to get interested in something, other than that useless Smithy kid." George gave her a stern look. "And I ain't kidding about that Mar, I see him around here again I'm gonna kick his ass so far up his behind, he'll look like a camel."

"Now George," Ruth looked at Randy, "What's your name again?"

Before Randy could respond, Marla said, "Dude, he's the dude."

"Shut up, Mar," Ruth scolded.

Randy blurted, "It's Randall, Randall Lupinski."

"You a Pollock?" George asked.

Randy wasn't sure how to respond. That question wasn't in the binder Scales gave him. "My father's parents were Eastern European."

"You go to college?" George continued his interrogation.

"I did my undergraduate work at Marquette and I am completing my graduate work at Notre Dame."

"See, Ruth, I knowed he was Catholic the minute he walked in here. It's okay son, you're among friends. This town can get a little seedy when it comes to religion. You get in the middle of that Baptist clutch, and they find out you're red, well, it could get a little sticky."

Randy felt something rubbing his leg under the table. He didn't remember seeing any little dog. Maybe it's the cat. Then he saw Marla had slumped down in her chair and was smiling, the tongue ring still exposed, the rub moving up his leg.

Randy pulled his feet back under his chair, but that just caused the errant foot to climb up between his knees. He could feel sweat beads forming on his forehead and his stomach was starting to roll.

George continued, "Mar here, she's talked about learning how to write books, poetry, stuff like that; tried to tell her, you can't buy beer with a worthless piece of paper with some words on it. She needs to learn how to do something with her hands."

"I already know how to do things with my hands," Marla responded looking directly at Randy and smiling.

"Oh yeah," George said sternly, "If you're so handy, why ain't you got a job?" George turned to Randy and answered his own question. "She ain't got a job 'cause there aren't any jobs that start at noon and end at three; where you don't have to wear clothes and there's no moving parts that could get hooked in one of those rings sticking out of her…., whatever."

Ruth spoke up, stubbing out one cigarette and reaching for another. "Now George, that's why Randall's here, so, what do you think Mar's qualified to do, or what kind of courses should she take?"

Finally, Randy thought, a question that's in the binder with a pat answer. "We specialize in placement, which means we analyze the qualities of the student, direct them in the educational process, and then guarantee job placement after graduation."

Marla slumped lower, twirling a curl with her finger and thrust her foot halfway up Randy's crotch.

Randy gulped, faked a cough, reaching for a non-existent handkerchief and grabbed Marla's foot, trying to force it away from his chair.

Ruth seemed concerned about Randy's reddening complexion. "Would you like something to drink, Randall, or maybe a Kleenex?"

"No thank you, Mrs. Todd," Randy rubbed some sweat from his forehead, and then felt the foot climbing his leg again. Maybe if he drew Marla's attention toward some other topic, other than his crotch, so he asked, "Marla, have you given this any thought, I mean, what would you like to study, or learn to do?"

Marla's aggressive foot seemed to relax as she strained to address the question.

Finally, she responded, "I was watching HGTV and, like, there's this babe that fixes up old houses. She wears these cool shorts and, like, a halter top, and has this holster with all kinds of tools in it. Like, I could do that. Does the school give you a tool holster?"

Great, another question in the binder and Randy smiled. "Yes, we do have a master carpenter course study. Jerry Featherstone teaches that course with actual on-site training."

"Jerry Featherstone?" George asked with astonishment. "I went to high school with him. I've know'd Jerry forever. Last I heard, he was bankrupt, stuck a bunch of people with half built houses."

Randy hesitated and then responded quietly, "Must be a different Jerry Featherstone."

George persisted, "Oh, there ain't two Jerry Featherstones around here, at least, let's hope not. Mom, you remember Jerry, don't you. He's the one blew up the old water tower at the train station." He turned back to Randy. "He thought it'd be neat to set off a pound of black powder on top of the old water tower on the fourth of July. It weren't used anymore, and he got it up there, alright, but, when it went off, the whole thing collapsed on top of the old train station. Yeah, I think he did six months in county for that."

The foot found its mark this time and Randy jumped out of his seat and abruptly stood. Both George and Ruth stared at

46

him with cigarettes dangling in open mouths. Randy adjusted his blazer and sat back down, this time scooting his chair out, away from the table, and crossed his legs.

"As I said," Randy continued, "Marla can learn carpentry, interior or exterior design, schematic recognition skills……"

"What?" George asked. "Schemmie what?"

"Schematic Recognition skills," Randy responded, pleased to have questions relating to his mission. "Essentially, she learns how to read blue prints, house plans, things like that."

"Oh," Ruth said, "that sounds interesting. What about that, Mar?"

Marla crossed her arms again, showing some attitude. "Do I get a tool holster?"

Time to close this deal, Randy thought. "I'm sure the tool holster is part of the curriculum." He pulled an enrollment contract out and laid it on the table. "Now, to get Marla enrolled and get her that tool holster, we need to complete the enrollment application. Once that's completed and we have a good faith deposit of five hundred dollars, we can start the student loan process, assuming you want to go that route."

"We don't do no loans," Ruth said puffing out a strong stream of smoke. "Marla's grandma left her some money, specifically for school, so we will be paying cash."

"That's my money," Marla said with conviction looking at Randy, "and they been holding out on me ever since she did the deep six."

"You watch your tongue young lady," Ruth said sternly.

Randy tried to mediate, "Well, now her wishes will come true." All of Marla's fooling around under the table had merely been a distraction up to this point, but the word cash gave Randy a chill and an immediate stimulation. "Let's just finish this paperwork," he said, smiling and pulling a pen out of his Armani sport coat.

CHAPTER 6

J im Scales sat at a round table in the Grill Room of the Hinkley Country Club nursing a gin and tonic while John White, C.E.O. of First State Bank, and Collin MacGregor, owner of Hinkley Building and Supply, finished their lunch. "How's the salmon?" Scales asked, more out of boredom than concern.

"Not bad, cooked a little too much, but overall, not bad." White took another bite.

"Since when are you some kind of gourmet food critique?" MacGregor asked, stuffing the last part of his hamburger in his mouth and waving at the waitress, pointing at his empty beer bottle. "How can you cook fish too much? What, you want it pink in the middle?"

Scales glanced at his watch. "Guys, I've got some appointments this afternoon, so what do you think of the offer?"

White immediately lost his concern about the quality of the salmon, holding a big chunk up in the air on his fork, like he was examining some sort of specimen. "I'm a little skeptical, myself. Asking the bank to finance a spec house is a little beyond our scope, if you know what I mean."

MacGregor almost reverted to a Scotch accent when he said, "And what's this stuff about wholesale? How am I supposed to stay in business selling you stuff wholesale?"

"You guys seem to be missing the point." Scales took a long draw on his drink and shook his head. "This is for the kids, teaching them a trade. And then when it's all done, you get your money back. Seems pretty simple to me; what's the old saying, no risk, no reward."

"Okay," White said pushing his plate to the side, "I get the risk part, I just don't get the reward part."

"Guys, just picture it," Scales held up his hands like a film director framing a shot, "a big sign in the front yard of the only new construction in Hinkley County; financed by First State Bank; building materials supplied by Hinkley Building and Supply; and in big letters, *for the good of our youth,* or some sappy line like that. You'll be the talk of the town, helping these poor kids learn a trade; local people helping local people, that's what it's all about."

"So, when it's done, ready to sell, who's going to buy it?" White asked. "I can't remember the last time a new house got built and put on the market. There's been a few built by some of the farmers, for their own use, but none for sale. And there's a good reason; you got to have a good job to do that, and there aren't any that I know of."

"Yeah," MacGregor, not the sharpest crayon in the box, tried to stay with the conversation and chimed in, "who's gonna buy it?"

"I don't think that will be a problem, I can guarantee it."

White and MacGregor looked at each other, and then back at Scales. White got a grin on his face. "You sneaky son of a bitch, you're gonna use these kids as slaves to build you a new house."

Scales feigned an objection to such a preposterous suggestion. "Why John, how could you say something like that, it's a learning experience."

All three were quiet for a minute, White pushing a napkin around his coffee cup and said slowly, "How many of these houses you plan on building?"

MacGregor, finally sensing where the conversation was going, added, "Yeah, how many, and how many of these *students* you got?"

"Well," Scales said with a slight smile, realizing the hook was set, "A semester is about four months and, depending on the size and design, given some weather consideration, and school holidays, I figure about eight months. Right now we have about twelve students in the master carpentry class, and should have a few more by the time we start fall. So, John, they could potentially start your house next summer. And Collin, that would put your start someplace late next year."

Collin took a draw on his beer. "How's come you get to go first?"

"Well, my friend, it's my school and they're my students. 'Nuff said?"

White and MacGregor looked at each other again.

White said, "I guess I could bring it up to the board, I mean, the loan part. The loan board would have to approve it, but, they pretty much follow my lead."

MacGregor took another draw on his beer, wiped his lips with his sleeve and said, "As long as I got a guarantee, I guess I can supply the materials. I'd have to add a handling fee, maybe five percent."

"Here's the second part of the deal that should make everything fall together. I have to have a board of directors for the school. I figure at least five, plus myself. So John, you can be Vice President and Collin," Scales rubbed his chin, "you can be Secretary."

"What," Collin said, choking on some of his beer, "I'm not gonna be nobody's secretary."

"It's just a title," Scales said emphatically. "The board needs a Vice and a treasurer, Rowena's agreed to do that, and a recording secretary. You don't have to do anything. And when it's your turn for a house, nobody's going to question the fact a hard working board member volunteered to reimburse the school."

MacGregor let that fact sink in and responded quietly, "Well, okay, but I don't want it spread all over that I'm a secretary."

Scales raised his empty glass signaling a toast. "It's agreed then. Welcome to the world of higher education. Anyone want an honorary master's degree?"

CHAPTER 7

Scales burst into Rowena's office, smiling like he just won the lottery and flopped down in one of her padded folding chairs.

"What's up boss, your wife just serve you papers?" Rowena said, sliding the crossword puzzle into her desk drawer.

"Sometimes I amaze myself, the ideas that come at the darn'dest times. I'm driving down Main Street, and I see Mary Beth Wilkins dropping her kid off at the Early Harvest Preschool; he's about three, I would guess. Anyway, I hadn't talked to her since the store closed, so I go over and gave her a little peck, just to renew old times."

"As I recall, you did a little more than peck, at least until Ray got wind of it. That kid don't have light hair, does he? They both got Indian in 'um, dark hair, not light, like yours."

"Oh no, he's dark, thank God. Anyway, she says the daycare is about eat'in 'em up. She works at the Dollar General now and Ray's still at the feed mill. I say, how much you have to pay? She says, two hundred a week. *Two hundred a week,* Rowena, can you imagine?"

"So, daycare's expensive, so what?"

"So what, she says.... So what about a certificate in, I don't know, Disciplines of Child Care, or, Doctrines of Preschool Management? We've got plenty of room out back for a fenced playground. Throw some swings up; put some sand in a tractor tire; that's all we need. Get ten students enrolled and open up for business. Twenty preschoolers at, let's say, one fifty a week, that's twelve grand a month; plus we get to charge tuition."

Rowena studied him for a moment, and then said, "And you put Joy Cummins out of business. Undercut her price with your free labor; that ain't fair."

"Are you talking about Professor Cummins?"

Rowena squeezed out a smile. "You are one slippery son of a gun, Dr. Scales."

Scales continued, "Joy said she would love to work here, not have to worry about all the small stuff," he was on a roll now, plotting out the next moves, "and she knows all the rules and licensing stuff. She said we would have to get inspected, that is, once we get Featherstone in here to do some remodeling. The kids have to have separate restrooms and stuff like that."

"Sounds expensive," Rowena said.

"Don't sweat the small stuff, that's my motto." He jumped up and said turning for the door, "I've got to get to the printer and get some brochures made up. I like the Doctrines of Preschool Management, what do you think?" He left without waiting for an answer, then stuck his head back in, "And have Lupinski call me right away. I need to fill him in so he can sell some......, I mean enroll some students in our new class."

54

*

Randy walked down the row of used cars at Frank's Auto World in Cougar Falls. He had driven by twice, noticing the BMW at the end of the row, but wanted to give the impression that he really wasn't interested by casually kicking every tire in the place before finally arriving at his target.

He had just enrolled his twenty fifth student in less than a month and was almost giddy with excitement over his bank account balance. He had moved out of the Hinkley Motor Inn and into a furnished apartment on the outskirt of Cougar Falls, some thirty miles from the school, intentionally giving himself some distance from the office and Jim Scales.

A tall, young looking salesman approached from a skirted trailer serving as the used car sales office. His cowboy boots and long sleeve plaid western style shirt didn't complement his blue polyester pants, and his handle bar mustache granted further concern about his reliability; but his pearly white smile assured that he found great satisfaction in a new customer.

"Howdy partner. Got your eye on that BMW I take it. My name's Jackson, folks call me Jack; what's yours?" Jack put his boot on the bumper of the next car and struck a casual pose with his elbow on his knee.

"Randall…., I don't know that I'm looking for a BMW, but I guess this one is pretty clean, how many miles?"

"Well, I'll tell you partner, I don't know that this one is available. I've had two offers on it already this morning. They both hustled out of here headin' for the bank. Last thing I yelled at 'um when they was rushin' outa here was, first one back with the cash, gets the car." Jack rubbed his chin. "I mean, if you're a cash buyer, well, you know, I'd probably have to let you have it, that's assumin' they don't come rushin' in here while we're foolin' around chit chattin'. You fixin' to trade, that it?" Jack strained to get a look at Randy's Honda, covered with road dust. "That your old Honda over there? Got a bunch of 'um on the lot already, not movin' too fast. "

Randy's cell phone chirped and he excused himself from the negotiation just in time to hear Rowena tell him Dr. Scales needed to see him right away.

"I'm in a meeting right now, but I'll call him as soon as I get done....... I know it's important, it's always important." He disconnected and turned his attention back to Jack, but Jack was headed back toward the office trailer. "Uh, Jack, where you going? What's the bottom dollar?"

Jack turned and said, "Oh, I didn't think you was too interested, so I was gonna go check on that other fella that went to the bank. But, I guess we could talk some more, if'n you are ready to deal."

Randy looked at the BMW, then at his phone, considering how much agitation he had been taking from Scales to enroll students, no matter what the circumstances, and held up his hand. "Hold on a minute Jack, I think I'm interested, well, I mean, I'm real interested. You think you can call that bank for me?"

CHAPTER 8

J im Scales called the first faculty meeting of the Hinkley Community College to order in the private meeting room of the Hinkley Country Club. Present were Rowena Ringwald, Dean of Girls and Professor of Business Curriculum; William Robert Redbone, commonly known as Billy Bob, Professor of Biological Sciences; Jerry Featherstone, Professor of Carpentry and Design; Buford Santini, commonly known as Buzz, owner of Buzz's Body Shop and Repair and Professor of Automotive Mechanics and Design; Joy Cummins, Professor of Preschool Management and Adolescent Child Care; and the newest addition, Lisa Calmwater, licensed massage therapist and co-owner of the *Bare Essentials* Gentleman's Club in Cougar Falls, Professor of Human Therapy Sciences and part time athletic director.

Scales held up his hand, requesting a reprieve from the group's indulgence in the spread of food and drinks he had provided. "Okay folks, let's get started. I've got some important announcements tonight, and….," he gave a dramatic pause for emphasis, "we've only got 2 weeks until classes start.

You all know and have met Randy Lupinski, our Admissions Administrator." Everyone turned and gave faux smiles to Randy. "He's been doing a bang-up job. We are now at eighty nine students. We'll top that one hundred mark, hopefully next week, that right Randy?"

Randy had a duck liver canapé just at mouth level when the question was asked, so he just shook his head in the affirmative.

"Now," Scales continued, "you can't have a successful school like this without a mascot and team name, even though we don't have any teams yet, but that's in the works too. Lisa has plans to start several intramural sports like ping pong, bowling; what else Lisa?"

Lisa grasped the chance to stand and expose her enhanced breasts to the attendees, only hidden by a see-through camisole and bikini bra. "Well," she started with an exhausted breath, "I've got a line on two pool tables from a bar that closed in the Falls, plus, there's enough room out back for a sand volley ball court; that's an Olympic sport, you know." Lisa put a finger to her lips, like she was tasting something sweet, trying to come up with additional ideas, but had apparently stumbled into a brain void, which was a common characteristic for her.

Scales took control. "Thanks, Lisa, I know you'll do a good job organizing things; can't wait to see you on that volley ball court. Like I said, can't have a vibrant school and enthusiastic students without a mascot and school team name. I've given this a lot of thought, but, it was tough to come up with something that wasn't already taken. I thought Hawks, but, as you know, that's already used by the high school. I went through several other bird names, cat names and so on; tried to stay away from Indian names to be politically correct," he glanced at Redbone, "and not offend our resident half breed, Billy Bob.....; went through about every other screwy name, like Illini, whatever that means. Then, I thought, how about the Fighting Owls? Owls are wise…; we like that; Owls are big and strong, at least in the bird world…; we like that. So, I throw this out to Lisa, since she's kind of in charge of the athletics, and she immediately says, how about the Hinkley Hooters?" Scales watched for any enthusiastic reaction, but only received blank stares.

"We'll have a mascot, an Owl, you know, a costume with feathers and a big beak." Scales held up his hand for the international sign of 'wait a minute' and went to the corner of the room and opened a big box. He quickly distributed a hat and tee-shirt to each person in the room. The hat had in script, Hinkley Hooters wrapped around the face of an Owl. The tee-shirt, a washed out green color, had the same insignia in large letters on the back and a smaller patch on a shirt pocket in the front.

With a big smile, he continued. "It's official, we're now the Hinkley Hooters. I can see it now," he held up his hand and made a panoramic sweep, "Hinkley Hooters, community college state champions….., of some sort; maybe baseball, or softball, something like that; something where you don't have to buy a bunch of equipment."

Rowena said quietly to Billy Bob beside her, "Something where you don't wear much clothes too, I bet."

"Now," Scales said, moving back to the head of the table, "let's get serious for a moment. Classes start in two weeks. That means you all have to have your class curriculum ready like we discussed. It needs to be collated into the binders I gave you for each student and I need a copy to keep on file for the accreditation committee." He looked around the room and could not meet anyone's eyes. "Buzz, you got yours ready?"

Santini had been leaning back, his hands clasped and resting on his stomach, trying to keep his eyes open after consuming four beers, but heard his name and leaned forward. "Huh, yeah I like hooters, they're great."

Scales sighed as everyone else chuckled. "Yeah, I bet you do. I asked if you have your curriculum ready, for your class?"

"Curriculum, what do I need curriculum for? You don't need no book to fix cars. You think the kid's gonna look at a book when I show him a bent fender? I'll give him a wrench and a blow torch, and then I'll let him figure it out for himself. You take broke parts off and put new parts on. That's the way I learnt. It ain't rocket science."

Billy Bob snorted, "That's for damn sure."

Buzz gave him a hard stare. "And what, cuttin' the guts out of a hog takes brains?"

Scales rubbed his forehead. "Alright guys, let it go. Buzz, we talked about this, remember? I told you, we'll use your shop as a classroom, but you have to come up with a written class plan." He looked at Lisa, and then back at Buzz. "How 'bout I send Lisa down to the shop tomorrow and the two of you put some notes together, get that book organized, sound like a plan?"

Buzz smiled, leaned forward and looked at Lisa. "Sounds like a plan to me. Maybe we could meet at your club. I ain't been there in a while."

Billie Bob remarked, "Since yesterday, I bet."

"Okay," Scales continued, "Randy, how many appointments you got set for tomorrow?"

Randy, who was sitting in the corner of the room, feeling somewhat aloof from the faculty, swallowed the shrimp he had just ingested with a gulp and said, "I've got a student and parents coming to the school in the morning; didn't pick up any leads from Rowena yet today, so there may be more."

"I want to be at that hundred mark by the end of the week. Do whatever you have to do, but get those students enrolled. We especially need some more kids in the day care program. Joy tells me there needs to be one adult for every five kids under the age of three in the nursery. We are still three short in that program, so steer some of the girls that way.

"Jerry," Scales turned his attention to Featherstone, "how's the negotiation going on that lot we looked at, the one next to number ten green?"

"The owner's still holding out," Featherstone said, holding a beer bottle in one hand, "wants the full twenty grand. Said he didn't give a crap about the fact the kids were learning how to build a house. I told him what you said, the thing about making a big deal about him donating the land, put a picture of him and his old lady on a sign. He said you could shove the sign up your...., anyway, he didn't go for it."

"Okay, maybe we wait a week or so. I can send White from the bank out there to put some pressure on him. They're kind of buddy buddy here at the club, if you know what I mean.

"Anyway, I've got even bigger news. You guys are going to love this. The State Department of Jobs and Family Services, the one in the capital, wants to do a commercial, of sorts, about our school starting up. They needed some kind of good news story to tell, you know, people getting retrained; kids finding themselves through education, stuff like that. Anyway, we're the only new start-up in the state. So, they called me and want to send some fancy Hollywood production company over here and do a touchy, feely, good news story that they can feed to the press. The lady that called me even said the Governor may show up; get his smiling face in front of the camera. She couldn't give me a date but said it would be soon. That means, whatever day it is, everyone's got to be dressed in their Sunday finest. I figure, we can do the student orientation day at the same time. Get a bunch of students in the building for good photo op's, if you know what I mean."

Buzz opened one eye and asked, "What's a photo pop, and, you mind if I order another beer?"

Scales rubbed his forehead. "Just show up without any grease on your clothes, okay Buzz. We might have you bring some tools and we'll get a shot of you showing some kids the ropes under the hood, taking a carburetor apart, something like that."

"Cars don't have no carburetors no more. See, that's the problem, nobody fixes nothin' anymore, they just stick some wires up the car's hind end and start changing parts. When I first got started......"

"Okay, Buzz, we get the picture. We'll still need you standing next to a car, pointing or something. These people are professionals; they'll come up with some interesting way to make you look good."

Redbone remarked, "Good luck with that."

Lisa's eyes were sparkling as she looked dreamily at the wall and then turned to Scales. "Is this, like, going to be on TV? For real?" Without thinking, she reached under her camisole and adjusted her bra straps. "Damn, I need to go shopping."

Redbone, Santini, Scales and Featherstone all quietly watched as she made some adjustments.

Rowena finally ended the silence. "Okay boys, the shows over. You mind Lisa, save it for your pole dance."

"I don't pole dance, well, not anymore," Lisa responded giving one last jiggle.

Scales cleared his throat. "Well, now you know what's on the agenda. We've got a lot going on and we are going to make history with our little college right here in Hinkley County. We might even be on the national news. You never know. Anyone have any questions?"

They all looked at each other and then Buzz spoke up. "Uh, can I get that beer to go?"

CHAPTER 9

The lingering smell of rotting vegetables had dissipated and as long as Randy kept a bottle of Lysol handy, he was able to tolerate his office. If a latent odor seeped up through the floor, he would give the area a good shot of disinfectant that stymied the insulting odor long enough to complete whatever task was at hand.

He maneuvered his selection of pens and pencils into an orderly row, opened the file for Mary Good and read the bio supplied by Jim Scales in anticipation of his appointment scheduled at one o'clock; ten minutes away, if his *Coke, the drink that refreshes*, clock was accurate.

Mary Good, daughter of Ralph and Audrey Good, farmer and homemaker, Mennonite heritage, only child, eighteen, recent graduate of Central Mennonite School, 4.0 grade average with no reference to future plans in the high school annual, no recorded mortgage on a six hundred acre grain and livestock farm.

He closed the folder just in time to look up and see Ralph Good standing in the door way staring at him. Ralph gave no indication of his vocation by his dress; a black suit, white shirt, skinny black tie, all hanging on a slim, bony frame. His hair line receded and was cut short, revealing only grey stubble. The only rugged feature was his well weathered face, with little or no expression, other than perhaps apprehension.

Randy broke the awkward moment and introduced himself. "I'm Randall Lupinski, Admissions Director for the school. You must be Ralph Good." Randy worked his way around the small desk and stuck out his hand.

Ralph ignored the greeting, glanced out the door and with a tilt of his head summoned the rest of his family into the office.

Mary Good took timid steps through the door, almost being pushed by her mother who had her hands on Mary's shoulders in step behind her. Both woman had hair nets tied under their chins, ankle length flowered dresses buttoned tight to their necks, and of course, no makeup or jewelry. Once assembled, they stood behind three chairs in front of Lupinski's desk, apparently waiting for instruction on what to do next.

Randy retreated back to his chair, still standing, and said, "Well, it's so nice to meet….. all of you…. the Good family, I mean. Well, shall we all sit down?" Another awkward second as Randy started to sit but the Goods didn't move, both women looking at Ralph for confirmation. Randy, halfway into the chair, stopped, as if he needed Ralph's permission as well, and waited. Finally, Ralph moved around his chair and sat, followed by the two women, giving Randy opportunity to drop into his chair.

Randy read from memory the first line of the sales manual. "Well, Mary, I understand you are interested in continuing your education. What are you interested in? We have a variety of vocational classes ranging from basic hands on experience, to highly technical training. Have you given this any thought?"

Once again silence enveloped the room.

Ralph finally spoke. "We are common folk Mr. Lupinski."

"Call me Randall," Randy said generating a big false smile.

"We are common folk Mr. Lupinski," Ralph began again, "and our women folk don't tend to need a lot of school learning. But Mary, well she's a little different."

Lupinski thought, *you got that right*, while he tried to hold back a yawn. He tried to remember if he had closed the windows on the BMW; didn't want a bunch of dust in the car. His yawn started to evolve into a chuckle, so he put his hand to his mouth for a fake cough. "Excuse me, a little tickle in my throat."

Ralph continued, "When I say different, I mean, she has a streak of smart that most in our family don't have. She's read more books in her few years than all the rest of us put together in our whole lifetime. She's able to figure stuff out, you know, just using her head, where I'd have to chew through three pencils, and still be scratching myself."

Mary and Mrs. Good sat stoic, staring at Randy with blank eyes, like they could hear the conversation, but their light switch was turned off.

"Anyway, me and the misses talked it over, and, well," he looked at Mary and then back at Randy, "we don't figure she's gonna get married anytime soon." There was a hint of disgust in his voice. "So, we thought she might as well get some more learnin'." Ralph finished the recitation with finality, like he had practiced the speech in the barn twenty times over.

Now all three stared at Randy without so much as a facial twitch.

"Well, I see," Randy said trying to redirect his thought process from what the dinner special might be at the Nite Owl Saloon, to getting a signature on the enrollment application and a check. "So Mary, do you have a special area of, shall we say, interest, like, do you want to be a teacher? Maybe you are interested in child care. We have a wonderful program for infant and adolescent child care. Sound like something you would like to experience?"

The wrinkles in Ralph's expressionless face tightened a bit. "That sounds exactly like what Mary would like to do. She's real good with the neighbor's kids."

Randy reached into a desk drawer and pulled out a tri-fold brochure and laid it in front of Mary. "This is a highlight of our Doctrines of Pre-School Management Program. It's a comprehensive course study, detailing not only the integral details of managing a pre-school environment, but also includes classes in business management as well." He paused, trying to think of the next line Scales had programmed into the sales pitch.

Ralph snatched the brochure with his leathery etched hand and gave it a cursory look. "She get some kind of degree out of this?"

"Each student that completes the study receives a certificate of completion along with the opportunities afforded by our

67

comprehensive job placement department. So far, we have a one hundred percent success rate." Randy had yet to have anyone ask how you could have one hundred percent success when the school hadn't officially graduated anyone. But he still felt a twitch when he said it, knowing it would be a tough question to counter.

Ralph looked at his wife, and then at Mary, who was staring at the floor, gave a little sucking sound, like he had something stuck in a tooth, then said, "I'd say that sounds like what Mary needs."

Audrey Good made the first noise since she entered the room by clearing her throat, an attempt to get Ralph's attention. "Oh Yeah," Ralph said after glancing in her direction, "Uh, you folks, well, you folks had any trouble with all this drug stuff? We don't want our Mary to be around a bunch of hooligans, the kind, well, the kind you see on TV, if you know what I mean."

"I'm glad you asked, Mr. Good. We have what we like to call a drug free campus; zero tolerance, if you know what I mean. Any of our students get caught even day dreaming about putting some foreign substance in their body and they are expelled, quicker than you can say marihuana. Dr. Scales, he's our President and source of inspiration, said right from the start, he wants this institution of higher learning to be placed on a pedestal, an example for other schools to aspire to. And I think we have accomplished that." Randy gave them a radiant smile and pulled an enrollment contract from his briefcase leaning against the desk."Now, all we need to do is get Mary enrolled, classes start next week, you know."

*

Randy pushed the completed and signed application, with check for first semester tuition, into his brief case and stood, holding out his hand to Ralph Good for the second time. This time Ralph shook the hand without any facial expression, creating an awkward moment when nothing was said and no one moved toward the door. Randy took the initiative and walked around the guests to the door, ushering them like lambs to the barn and into the hall.

At the end of the hall the room opened up, exposing the large windows across the front of the converted grocery store. As Randy led them down the hall he made small talk about the large number of students taking advantage of the educational opportunities afforded by Hinkley Community College and how the social experience would be one Mary would long cherish. As he turned to slap Ralph one last time on the back and push him toward the exit, he saw Marla Todd leaning against a post just outside the main entrance, entertaining two males, both sporting gang leathers, bandanas and blue jeans with more holes than a piece of Swiss cheese. Marla had on a skimpy skin tight halter top with a chain suspended between the outlines of her nipples; low rider short shorts exposing numerous tattoos and other body piercings, and it looked like they were passing around a joint.

Instead of slapping Ralph on the back, he wrapped his arm around his shoulders and made him take a hard left turn away from the exit. "I just thought of something, I'm sure you all would like to see the, uh, the…. the day care center, yeah, the

day care center where Mary will be spending a lot of her time…
learning about day care. Let's just go this way."

The day care center was under construction and was
located where the walk in freezer had been, near the back of
the building. The plan called for a direct exit to the, yet to be
constructed, fenced playground.

The group wound their way through unorganized tables and
chairs, portable office partition walls, and mounds of discarded,
spent building materials.

"Watch your step," Randy instructed, "we're in the final
stages of construction, getting ready for the first day of class."

Ralph led the two women in a line behind Randy and he
said in a matter of fact manner, "Looks like there's quite a bit
left to do."

Randy opened the unpainted door in a partition wall, hoping
to find some semblance of order in the under construction child
care center. Sitting on a board suspended between two saw
horses were Jerry Featherstone and another worker, each with a
beer in their hand, laughing like they had just been entertained
by a stand-up comic.

They both turned and looked at Randy and Featherstone
said, "Lupinski, come on in, you want a beer?"

Randy slammed the door shut, backing into Ralph, who
in turn backed into his wife and she caused Mary to lose her
balance and fall in a pile of saw dust. All three reached out to
help Mary regain her footing and brush the saw dust from her
long dress.

"Construction workers," Randy said with a sheepish smile,
"you never know what they're gonna do, and I forgot, this is

a hard hat zone." Randy padded himself on the head. "Don't want to get whacked on the noggin."

Randy slowly turned the group and headed back toward the front of the building, trying to formulate plan B, assuming the undesirables were still loitering near the door, but it appeared they had finished their shared moment of spiritual enlightenment and moved on. He breathed a sigh of relief and moved quickly toward the exit, hoping to get the Goods on their way before any other negative impressions could be encountered.

Ralph led the women out of the door and turned to Randy; Randy expecting him to ask for his tuition payment back. Instead Ralph said passively but with strong intent, "Mr. Lupinski, the wife and I are counting on you to watch out for our Mary. She ain't used to the big city and the things that go along with it. She's a good girl, well, I mean she *is* a Good," he cracked a smile, the first Randy had seen since their first meeting, "but she's also a good girl, the kind that could easily be steered wrong, if you know what I mean. So, we are counting on you to keep an eye on her. We got an understanding, Mr. Lupinski?"

Suddenly Randy saw another side of the lean, leather skinned Ralph Good. He saw or imagined a lean leather skinned Ralph Good coming after him with a shot gun or some other lethal farm utensil because his Mary came home with a tattoo on her butt, or worse yet, with one of the low life's that were loitering just minutes ago where he now stood. In the last month he had been confronted with numerous unusual requests by doting parents, but this was the first request for him to be a surrogate in their stead.

71

With apprehension, Randy said, "I'm sure she'll do just fine." Then he had a thought that might relieve their fear and transfer the responsibility to someone else. "I'll put a *Good*," Randy smiled and raised his hands signaling parenthesis on the word good, "word in with Rowena Ringwald, our Dean of Girls, to keep an eye out for Mary. That way, if she ever has any problems, she'll have someone to talk to, more on her level, if you know what I mean."

Ralph's steely eyes were still fixed on Randy. "I asked if *we* have an understanding, Mr. Lupinski?"

Randy gulped in a breath, looked at Mary, who was still staring at her feet, and replied without much emotion, "Yeah, I guess we do."

CHAPTER 10

The Governor sat at his desk, Mont Blanc fountain pen in hand, smiling like he was in a Crest commercial, waiting for the photographer to finish the photo session. With each "Okay" from the photographer, another group of suck up supporters would step behind the desk and smile for the camera, hoping their moment of fame would be the one printed in the Tribune's political section of Sunday's paper.

Finally, the Governor scribbled his name on the legislative document, cementing into law another unfunded mandate granting special property, income and sales tax exemption to private schools that, as was so eloquently stated in his preamble to the signing, at minimal profit paved the way for Illinois's future generations.

Jim Scales and Rowena Ringwald had elbowed their way into the final photograph, positioned directly behind the Governor; Scales at the last second placing his hand on the Gov's shoulder like they were best of friends. The flash ignited and almost as instantly, a plainclothes guard grabbed Scales and wrenched his arm behind his back shoving him away from the Governor and into an unoccupied corner of the office.

"You don't touch the Gov'," the guard said without moving his lips. His grab and hold maneuver was so slick, Rowena had hardly noticed, assuming Scales had stepped away on his own.

The Governor stood, signaling the end of the photo op, brushed imaginary lint off his shoulder and briskly walked out of the office, just as quickly followed by the guards, leaving Scales standing in the corner, checking to make sure he had not wet himself.

Rowena strolled over and said, "I thought you were gonna get some private time with the Gov', isn't that what you said? He owed it to you after that big donation. Talk about the commercial they are gonna make at the school. You feel alright? You look a little pale."

Scales nonchalantly adjusted his suit coat, regaining composure and said, "He musta had another meeting. Let's get out of here. I need a drink."

They turned to follow the rest of the crowd out into the large hall and a hand grasp Scales arm from behind.

Scales turned, expecting to see the big guard with the wire sticking out of his ear and said, "I didn't mean to touch him. Christ, he's just the Governor. What's the big deal?"

The young man stepped back, surprised at the outburst and held up his hands to fend off any offensive move by Scales.

"Oh, I thought you were the....., I thought, well, who are you?" Scales again composed himself, adjusting his shirt cuffs like the guy had caused some wrinkles.

"I'm Chad Overstreet, Assistant Secretary to the Governor. The Governor asked me to express his disappointment that he couldn't meet personally with you, but unfortunately, he was called away for another emergency meeting at the capital to meet with the Chairman of the appropriations committee. The deficits seem to just keep growing, no matter what we do."

Overstreet put on a big smile and continued, appearing more relaxed. "Now, how are we coming on the *big show,* so to speak; the commercial? I know we had to postpone the shooting because of construction, wasn't it? How's that coming? Are we about ready now? We would really like to get this in the can."

Scales looked at Rowena, and then back at Overstreet. "I wouldn't exactly say construction was the main problem. Your so called team of experts showed up, without an appointment I might add, walked around for fifteen minutes, and left. Said our school wasn't quite up to their expectations. So Chad…"

Overstreet interrupted, holding up his hand. "Okay, a little misunderstanding, I think. Since then, we've made some changes; hired a new advertising agency to be exact. So, I think things will go a little smoother this time. I plan on being there to personally oversee the shoot. Assuming the Governor can fit it into his schedule, he'll copter in for a quick interview and be part of the shoot. Sound good?"

"When's all this going to take place? I need a little advance notice to have the right people available," Scales said starting to relax.

Rowena said under her breath, "Yeah, we got to make sure Lisa's pole is set up."

Overstreet said, "What was that?"

Scales gave her a sharp stare and turned back to Overstreet. "An inside joke, how soon?"

"I'll try to get everything arranged for next week, but it could be the week after. Just depends on how soon I can get all the publicity set up and of course, the Governor's schedule. How is the campus looking? We'll want to see some students sitting outside, on a bench, something like that. Then, maybe the Governor conversing with some students, looking at their lab experiments, stuff like that"

"Yeah, lab experiments," Scales responded dryly. "We'll have a bunch of those."

Rowena couldn't help herself, trying to stifle a laugh, sounding more like a squeak or a sneeze. She had to walk away before she totally burst into laughter.

Overstreet watched her walk away and said, "She going to be alright, sounds like she may be choking?"

Scales maneuvered himself in front of Overstreet. "She's fine, probably a hair ball or something. Now, once this thing is completed, where's it gonna air. Are we talking local news, state, or what?"

Overstreet kept looking over Scales shoulder at Rowena, either concerned or maybe just interested in the hairball theory and whether it was going to reveal itself. He looked back at Scales. "Oh, you mean the commercial, or PSA?"

"PS what?" Scales asked.

"Public service announcement, it's like a commercial, only the stations run them for free. You know, when they can't sell the air time, they'll use a PSA to fill the schedule. It's an opportunity for us to get the Governor's face on the screen for free, and also tell a story about the great work he's doing."

That statement almost caused Scales to choke up his own hairball. With three current investigations in progress for purported misuse of campaign funds along with an unverified news leak that the Governor was having an affair with a college intern on his staff, he doubted a so called PSA would get much air time, and if it did, he wasn't sure he wanted the college as the backdrop.

Overstreet glanced at his Rolex. "Well, I've got to get back to my office, work on this schedule. You sure she's alright?"

Scales grabbed Overstreet's arm this time, and held his stare. "You telling me after all this screwing around, all this is gonna be is a piece of crap commercial that may or may not get put on after the late night show?"

"No, no, that's not exactly true. We'll get some initial publicity; I'll make sure of that. The PSA has more legs though, it'll be around for a while. It's more than news, it's a statement about the condition of our educational system, and how we need more money to keep moving in the right direction."

The mention of more money brought Scales temper under control and he said, "Okay, but I want…."

Overstreet shook loose of Scales grasp and quickly stepped away, saying over his shoulder, "I'll be in touch."

*

Scales swirled the swizzle stick in his martini, sitting in the bar of the hotel, trying to stab an olive.

77

Rowena wrapped a bar napkin around her beer bottle to absorb the condensation and said, "You see how she looked at me when I said I didn't want a glass? So what if I don't like to drink out of some fancy beer glass, what's it to her?"

Scales said slowly staring at his glass, "You know Row, here we are in this fancy bar, next to the capital building, where they spend billions of dollars and don't care; wear thousand dollar suits and ride around in limos; eat sushi and caviar for lunch; and just think, a year ago we would have been thinking about how to move two hundred pounds of bananas before they got too ripe. We've come a long way baby." With that said, he raised his glass to toast their achievement."

Rowena gave him the evil eye. "You aren't gonna try to hit on me, are you. Jerry told me to watch out, you get one of those, those silver bullets in you, no tellin' what you might do."

"Come on Row, I'm not gonna hit on you; after all these years together, geez. No, I'm just saying, we've come a long way; the store closing; the school; hell, the money. You're happy about that, aren't you? You make twice as much as you did at the store."

"Well, sure, I'm happy about that. But I also learned my lesson; nothin's forever. Twenty two years at the store and smack, the door hits you in the ass and that's it." She took a big swig of her beer, belched into her hand and continued. "I trust you and all that, but, I also know this whole thing could fall apart tomorrow. Come on Jim, your athletic director is a former stripper, and to be honest, I'm not sure about the former part. I know you are having fun playing doctor or professor, or whatever, but let's get real, at some point, these kids are gonna start asking about the jobs you promised. What then?"

Scales tried to look shocked, and then straightened his shoulders, resting an elbow on the back of his chair and faced Rowena. "I don't believe I ever promised anything, but, that's not the point. The point is we offer a service, a needed service, by everyone's estimation. We give these kids some direction in their lives. You ever see that girl that sits out in the lounge, the one with the tattoos and rings all over her body; the one that wears the contractor's tool thing all the time? Tell me she isn't getting her life straightened out."

"You talking about *Marla*, Marla Todd? You know what she has in that tool belt? Probably not, you're too busy looking at her ass sticking out of those shorts. That's where she carries her stash; her pot; what she sells to the other kids you are guiding through the turmoil of juvenile delinquency. Open your eyes Jim." Rowena blew out a sigh and took another swig.

Scales couldn't think of an appropriate rebuttal so he ventured on to another subject. "So, we're almost through our first semester, the building is shaping up, things look pretty good, don't you think?"

"What do you want, me to slap you on the back and sing the Hinkley Hooters' fight song?" She thought for a second and said, "We got one of those? If we do, it's probably something you can pole dance to. No Jim, You're right, you have come a long way, in what, a little over a year? But I still get queasy every time I walk in that building; kind of like the willies, you know what I mean? It just don't feel right some times."

Scales gave her the squint eye. "What do you mean, it don't feel right? You mean I don't have the heat turned up enough?"

79

Rowena shook her head. "No, I mean, here you…, we are taking all of this money from these kids, and them hoping they are going to get some great job… And you and me both know that ain't gonna happen. I'm just sayin', sometimes it just don't seem right, that's all….. Aw, just forget I said that. Just forget it."

"No, go on. Get it off your chest. I'm not saying I agree with you, but, maybe you have some suggestions, that what you're getting at? You have some new types of classes we can start, that will get the kids a job?" Scales lifted his martini glass in the direction of the bar keep, signaling for a refill. "Want another beer?"

"God no, I'll be peeing every fifteen minutes on the way home the way it is. No, I don't have any suggestions, well, about new classes anyway. It's just, you know…. For example," she turned to Scales, getting more serious, "You give Randy this handbook, the hard sell, get 'em to sign and in the door any way you can sales pitch. That's what I'm talking about. Half these kids, probably more than half don't give a hoot, pardon the pun, if that's what it is, about going to school. The one's that got school loans don't realize that they have to pay it back. It just gives them someplace to hang out, like still being in high school but without having to do any homework. Then the one's that do show up, thinking they are going to get an education, we put them to work babysitting, or building you a house, or fixing Buzz's customer's cars. Sometimes it just don't feel right. That's all I'm saying."

Scales nursed his martini, twirling the stuck olives around the rim. "Row, I was brought up in a house that, if we had breakfast, it was a slice of bread with some sugar on top, if we had some sugar, and maybe a glass of milk. And, we only had milk if the milkman was feeling generous enough to give us another week of credit. My pop worked about every job nobody else would do, at least for a week or two, and then he would take off and we wouldn't see him until the money was gone, and then he'd come home meaner that a sow grizzly.

"I learned real early that if I wanted anything, I had to go out and get it on my own. That's how I got started with Roush, in his original store in the Falls, as a bagger, working after school and weekends."

Rowena had heard this story at least fifteen times before; the alcohol induced self pity rant about how I had to do it all by myself. So she interrupted. "I can appreciate your need to succeed, Jim, but at what and who's expense, that's what I'm talking about. Oh, just forget it. You ready to go?"

Scales slurped down the remainder of his martini. "You sure you don't want to get a room?"

Rowena's jaw dropped and she was ready to pop Scales in the forehead with the beer bottle.

Scales held up his hands in defense with a big grin. "Just kidding Row, just kidding. Let's go before the traffic gets too bad."

CHAPTER 11

The faculty of Hinkley Community College had rounded out at ten full time instructors and three part-time. George Ratsner, former owner of Ratsner's Plumbing and Heating was added to teach the Fundamentals of HVAC. River Jones, a previously unemployed wildcatter and Jim Scales nephew, was added to teach the Fundamentals of Pipefitting or Welding Your Way to Riches, depending on who you asked. Ruth Bell, who published her own fictional novel called Dirty Dollars, about a dirt farmer that won the Illinois lottery and ended up turning his riches over to God and the Baptist church and working in a soup kitchen, instructed an adult night class in contemporary writing called the Art of Wordworking.

With the exception of the Welding class, because there wasn't any welding equipment available except for the arc welder permanently attached to Jones' old pickup truck and the weather had turned unsympathetic to outdoor activities, the classes, though lightly attended, were well funded by tuition from less than enthusiastic students, much to the credit of Randall Lupinski's increasingly successful sales ability.

The first semester was drawing to a close with everyone anticipating the Christmas and New Year break. Scales called a meeting of the faculty to trumpet the school's early successes and in several cases, garner explanations for some of the lesser publicized incidents of faculty indiscretion.

Scales called the meeting to order after a lengthy cocktail hour that included a tour of his new home adjacent to the tenth hole's green of the Hinkley Country Club. With the exception of some minor decorating touches, the house was completed just in time for the final exam consisting of his inspection of the work and the awarding of an A for every student that showed up for class at the work site at least eighty percent of the time.

Considering the free labor, discounted building materials and fifty percent donation of the lot cost, he had about One Hundred and thirty thousand dollars invested in what would be, after the in ground pool was installed, that being next semester's project, about a half million dollar luxury home.

"Okay folks, I'll make this brief. I know everyone wants to get home for the Monday night game. It's been a great first semester. I know we got off to a rocky start; that thing about the drug bust in the parking lot was unfortunate, but it taught us all a lesson. And the mix-up with the bad batch of meat in the child care lunches, well, that could have happened to anyone. The important thing is we now have one hundred and eighty three students registered for the winter session and only had eighteen that dropped out so far.

"And here's the good news, actually, great news. I have been working with the Accreditation Board for the past three months and, although it's not official yet, they have assured me we will be designated a level two institution within the next few weeks, meaning, we will be able to offer an actual Associates degree once the curriculum is approved and the student meets all of the requirements."

"Associates degree in what?" Billy Bob Redbone asked slightly slurring his words.

"I'm still working on that, but we will start with something workable, like business administration, or human resources, something like that. Randy Lupinski has tentatively agreed to step up to the plate and be our Professor and Dean of the Business School. He will finish his Master's degree in another month from Notre Dame adding a pillar of credibility we have been somewhat lacking."

Rowena, on her third beer asked, "Why don't you just make him a doctor, or something emeritus, whatever that is. That should give you a bunch of credibility."

Buzz Santini bounced his beer bottle on the table top drawing attention and asked, "When you gonna make me a doctor? I been poundin' out dents for thirty years, that should account for something. Ain't that credible?"

Billy Bob Redbone said, "Buzz is right. We ought to all be doctors."

Lisa Calmwater said, "I want to be a proctologist. Can you do that?"

Rowena slapped herself in the forehead. "Uh, Lisa, we aren't talking medical doctors here, but I'm sure you've had enough experience in that area to qualify."

Scales, sensing things were getting out of hand interrupted the banter. "Look, I appreciate you are working hard, and maybe at some point in the future, we can award some faculty advanced learning degrees, but right now we just need to keep moving in the right direction; keep focused on the future."

Buzz was on a roll and felt he had the crowd in his favor. "Jim, the way I see it, all the focus is on you. You got yourself a new house; a fancy company car; a big doctor title, like you's been to some fancy school or something; while the rest of us babysit a bunch of spoiled, pot smokin' retards. All I'm sayin' is, why ain't we doctors too?"

There were a couple of, "Yeh's," from the crowd and a, "Bein' a doctor ain't asking that much."

Scales could feel the burn rising in his gut, like when a customer would bring back a three quarter eaten watermelon and want money back because it wasn't sweet enough. He wandered away from the front table and stood next to Buzz.

"Buzz, how much did you make pounding dents last year?"

"Ain't none of your bidness. I done alright. I always done alright in the shop." Buzz looked around the room. "People know I do good work."

"Yeah, you do good work. But I would venture to say your income has more than doubled since you joined the school… Just put that new sun room on your house, looks nice too. Saw you carting that sixty inch TV home the other day." Scales bent down getting in Buzz's face. "But, that's not good enough, is it? Now you want to be a doctor. Of what, *dents*? A doctor of *dents*?" This drew a laugh but Scales could see Buzz was gripping his beer bottle so hard his fist was turning white. He stepped back out of harm's way.

"Look folks, this is supposed to be a happy occasion. We are making a name for ourselves. Hinkley Community College is starting to be respected as a credible institution of higher learning. That's *something*; I mean, *really something*. And you are all part of it. You should be proud. You should be strutting when you have on your Hooter tee shirt or hat."

Rowena almost choked on her last swig of beer when scales mentioned the Hooter tee shirt.

He noted her distress and continued. "Okay, the Hooter name may have been a bad choice, but it's something we have to live with now. I'm just telling you, you don't need some initials in front or in back of your name. The fact that you are associated with Hinkley College puts you above the rest. Be proud, you should be."

Scales walked back to the front table, opened a manila envelope and pulled out a stack of checks. "And to show how proud I am of each of you, I have a little something for you to put in your Christmas stocking. And don't worry, they are all for the same amount, so there's no use going around asking how much." As he moved around the room distributing the checks he said, "So, enjoy your break and fine tune your lesson plans for the next semester. It should be easier the second time around. And for those of you who have been assigned new class duties for second semester students, I need your study guides in my office within the next ten days. Have a great holiday and keep in touch."

The room started to clear and Rowena stepped next to Scales. "I thought for a minute there Buzz was gonna take your head off."

"Yeah, thanks a lot. It was your comment that got them all going about being doctors. Christ, can you imagine, Buzz Santini a doctor of something?"

Rowena smiled. "The doctor of dents thing was pretty funny, at least everyone but Buzz thought so. Oh well, the checks will make them forget about it, that's for sure."

"Let's hope."

CHAPTER 12

Most of the students were on break so the building was unoccupied, with exception of the day care, which continued operation through the holidays. The students that volunteered to work were paid minimum wage under the agreement the compensation would be deducted from future tuition.

Rowena manned the phones and did busy work in her office each morning, hanging the closed sign at noon. She was about to wrap up her morning when she heard a faint knocking on her office door.

"Yes, who is it? You can come in, it's open." She slid her crossword puzzle book into the desk drawer and waited. No answer. Suspicious and now a little frightened, realizing she was probably alone in the front part of the building, she opened a lower desk drawer and took out a hammer she used to hang pictures and cautiously stepped toward the door. "Who's there, anybody?"

She raised the hammer, keeping it hidden behind the door and slowly turned the handle, releasing the latch. Mary Good stood outside the door, staring at her bare feet, mostly hidden under her ankle length dress. Rowena eased the hammer down and held it concealed behind her, fully opening the door.

"Uh, may I help you?" She tried to put the face with a name, but it wouldn't come. She had heard about the introverted girl working in the day care that dressed like a Quaker and seemed to lack any social skills, but was excellent with the children. She softened her tone. "Can I help you with something? What's your name?"

"I'm Mary Good, I mean, my name's Mary Good." The reply was so subdued, Rowena could hardly hear.

"Okay Mary, that's a start. Come in. I don't get many visitors when the school is on break. Do you help in the day care?" Rowena closed the door behind Mary and returned to her seat. Mary continued standing just inside the door. "You can sit down."

Mary obeyed, sitting in the chair in front of the desk, still staring at her bare feet.

Rowena, perplexed, if not astonished at the girl's timidity, almost like it was contrived, tried to restart the conversation, "How are things in the day care? By the way, where are your shoes?"

Mary at least looked up, but still did not respond. A tear trickled down one cheek.

Rowena thought, oh boy, here we go. "Well, apparently we have some kind of problem here. You want to give me some direction. Somebody steal your shoes?"

Mary looked back down and said, "I don't wear shoes, except on Sunday, Papa thinks it's a waste."

"Oh, I see; I mean, it's freezing outside, but, who am I to criticize. Sooooo...." She drew out the transition in exasperation. "Is there some other issue we need to discuss?" Rowena nonchalantly looked at her watch.

"Dr. Scales said if I ever had a problem, I was to talk to you."

"Okay, he does say stuff like that once in a while, but if you would like to talk to him directly, I can call him." Mary reached for the phone, half smiling, thinking about how nice it will be dragging Scales butt down to the school to talk to some student who has menstruation problems or something.

"He said to talk to you. And my Papa said I should talk to you."

Mary slowly hung up the phone. "Well, here we are; what is it you want to discuss? It isn't, like, personal hygiene or something is it? Or pregnancy is it; you pregnant?"

Now both cheeks turned red.

"That's it, isn't it? One of these jokers knocked you up. Does *Papa* know?" Rowena's temperature was rising as she tried to envision which of the low life, tattooed, pot smoking students nailed Mary in the janitor's closet. And worse, Papa was probably a big farmer who would come down and tear the place apart looking for the loser.

"I'm not *pregnant*."

Rowena slumped back in her chair. "Thank God for that..... At least now we know this can't be too bad. Let's hear it."

Mary rubbed her nose on her dress sleeve and looked Rowena in the eye for the first time. "My Papa told me I had to come here and learn something. He wants me to be the first Good to have a degree." Mary stared into her folded hands. "Our religious belief is that a woman should stay in the house and have children and tend the farm. If a man wants to get an education, it's his decision, but a woman can't decide on her own. My Papa turned against the Elders and decided I was going to get educated. See, I don't have any brothers, so Papa won't have anyone to leave the farm, and, well, I guess he didn't think I would attract a good husband." Mary rubbed her nose again, like she was plotting the next phase of her story.

Mary started again, "Anyway,...."

The door jarred open and Billy Bob Redbone pushed through. He smiled at Rowena and started to say something and then noticed Mary in the chair. "Hey sis, how you doin'..... Where's your shoes?" He looked at Rowena and then back at Mary. "I interrupting something?"

"What do you think, Billy Bob? You forgot how to knock? What do you want?" Rowena said with some attitude.

"You got the checks? I could sure use it."

"Payday's not 'til Friday, you know that. Do you mind, we're having a private conversation here."

Billy Bob gave Rowena a 'whatever' look, turned and said, "See ya sis. Better find some shoes, I think it's gonna snow. Nice bonnet, by the way."

Rowena rose and sternly said, "Get out." The door closed and she said, "Sorry, he's a little crass at times. Don't mean nothing. Where were we?"

Mary continued like there was no interruption and the recitation had been rehearsed. "Papa thought I would be in class, reading, having to study, take exams. Instead, I'm working in a day care. Don't get me wrong, I like working with children, and sometimes, Mrs. Cummins shows me how the licensing is done and what the State inspector will be looking for and what to hide. But so far, we haven't had any written material to review and there hasn't been any real class work. I know next semester I am enrolled in Business Essentials and they said there may be a computer class at some point, but this just doesn't seem like a real college to me."

Rowena thought, I warned him, someday there would be someone who really wanted to learn something. "I understand, I think, but we are kind of a vocational college; hands on learning, so to speak. We try to put the student in a real life job environment. Now in your case, once you learn the ins and outs of running a real day care, and take a few more classes, you'll receive a certificate of some sort, almost like a diploma." Rowena rubbed her forehead. She was getting in deeper with each attempt to explain their mission. "Didn't Mr. Lupinski explain all of this?"

Mary looked up, rubbed her nose again and crossed her arms, the first visible sign of emotional attitude, besides tears. "So, the whole idea of this is to have me work in a day care while I, we pay tuition; is that it?"

Rowena looked at the squinting eyes and wondered where the timid girl went. "Well, I don't think…."

"That's the way it looks to me."

"Maybe you should talk to Dr. Scales. He could…"

"They told me to talk to you."

"Okay, I got that. What do you want me to do? I can talk to your teacher. I'm sure she can assign some extra work of some sort." Rowena straightened her desk pad and rearranged a pencil holder; looked at her watch again. "It's getting past noon. We usually close the office at noon."

Mary still had her arms crossed and didn't move.

Rowena coughed, rubbed her nose, looked at her watch again and fidgeted in her seat.

Mary said, "You remember when some of the kids got sick from eating the lunch meat?"

"Oh yeah, that was a shame. What a mess; all that vomit."

"Do you know why the meat was spoiled? You know where it came from?"

Rowena didn't have an answer, so she just shrugged her shoulders.

"My teacher, Mrs. Cummins, buys the food at an outlet store in Cougar Falls. It's a place where they send all of the out of date groceries, day old bread, and….. *out of date processed meats*. You know why I know that?"

Rowena's eyes were burning from not blinking while she listened in amazement. She shook her head.

"I know because we buy a lot of their stuff to feed our hogs and I saw the hand written receipt they give you. You can buy the stuff by the pound." Mary folded her hands in her lap. "Do you know where Mrs. Cummins hides the stuff she doesn't want the state inspector to see?"

Rowena, looking more sheepish by the second, again shook her head.

"I do."

"I really think you should talk to Dr. Scales."

Mary said, "You mean Mr. Scales. We both know he's not a doctor. I checked him out on the internet. He never even went to college. No, I don't want to talk to Mr. Scales." Mary rose from the chair, pulled her bonnet off and shook her hair loose until it fell around her shoulders. "I think you will talk to Mr. Scales, and the two of you will decide how I am going to get a degree, a real degree."

Mary walked to the door and turned, "Thank you for your time Mrs. Ringwald, I feel a lot better now."

CHAPTER 13

W hen the Super Value grocery store closed, every usable appliance and furnishing was removed, save those that were so permanently attached to the building that removal would have required demolition. The meat counter and cutting room, located in the rear of the store were disassembled, leaving only a walk-in cooler and numerous blood stains embedded in the concrete floor. The cutting or butchering room was partitioned with glass windows, allowing customers to view the blood soaked apron adorned butchers slice, dice and package the daily offerings.

The glass partitioned room offered an excellent setting for the college's so called biology lab, or it could be better described as the classroom assigned to the closest curriculum to biological science advertised as Anatomical Bovine Dissection Skills 101; or Keys to Profitable Retail Butchering; or How to Make Hamburger Out of Dated Case Meat, depending on who you asked.

Professor Billy Bob Redbone spent the winter break honing his teaching skills playing roulette at the Olatagwa Casino and running a handsome tab at *Bare Essentials* gentlemens club in

Cougar Falls. He did manage to coerce his sister, an English Literature teacher at Hinkley High School, to construct a lesson plan for the winter semester. The plan was so concise and well written that Dr. Scales used it as a template for the majority of the semester's class offerings.

Six students signed up for the Anatomical Bovine Dissection Skills course and they were seated in the cool, glass enclosed lab, waiting for Billy Bob to make his entrance. As usual, he was late arriving after an evening of clubbing.

Billy Bob pushed the lab door open, slamming it against the back of a student's chair, occupied by the only female attendant, Marla Todd. She signed up for the class under the assumption it had something to do with human anatomy, conjuring that opinion from the word anatomical in the class heading. She assumed bovine might be a derivative of booty, or behind, and dissection must be referring to the common practice of putting day-glow coloring in sections of your hair. Although her interest in construction had faded when the realization hit that it actually involved manual labor, she still wore her tool belt over stretch jeans with a low cut sweater allowing maximum viewing of her cleavage tattoo.

Marla bumped out of the chair and said, "Hey, watch it, jerk off."

Billy Bob, trying to focus through the blurry haze of blood enveloping his eyeballs responded, "If it ain't the pop top girl. How many of those rings you got we can't see?"

The other five male students all gawked, waiting for Marla to do show and tell. Instead, she retook her seat and folded her arms. "Ain't nobody in *this* room ever gonna find out, that's a fact."

Billy Bob moved to the front of the lab and pushed himself up on a stainless steel butcher's table. In doing so, he noticed the stain on the front of his jeans and wondered where it came from; *cheap tequila*, he thought. He slid his hand over his face, hoping the throbbing would soon dissipate. "So, you all are thinking maybe you want to get into the slaughterin' business, that it?"

Marla scrunched her nose. "The what?"

"Slaughterin'; butcherin'; cutting meat. It ain't a bad vocation, sissy. Ain't many women got the, the…," he thought balls but blurted out, "stomach for it."

"That what this is," Marla asked, "Learning how to cut meat?"

"What'd you think it was, a tattoo clinic?" This drew a laugh from the rest of the class. "Like I said sis, maybe you ain't got the stomach for it," Billy Bob said with a sly grin.

Marla wasn't one to back down from a challenge, especially from some middle aged drunk. "I've got plenty of stomach. At least mine doesn't hang over my belt like yours." This drew an equal chuckle from what now had become an audience.

Billy Bob sucked in a breath, trying to hide the bulge, and immediately got dizzy and had to stabilize himself on the table. "Well, sis, you're in luck today. I usually don't get into the real meat of the subject this soon; that's a little slaughterhouse punt," he smiled at his own joke.

"You mean pun; it's a pun, not a punt you putz." Marla said and then thought, *what a freaking idiot.*

Billy Bob didn't appreciate the correction. "You think you're pretty damn smart, huh, sis? You got a butcher knife in that tool belt? You're gonna need one. Like I said, I usually don't start the class with hands on demonstrations, but, little sis here seems to want to get her hands bloody."

Billie Bob slowly slipped off the table, regained his balance, and walked toward the walk-in cooler at the rear of the room built into the cement block wall. He whistled an indistinguishable tune as he walked, disappearing into the cavernous cooler with a resounding clunk of the thick door. He soon exited pulling a large stainless steel cart with a large carcass lying stiffly on top with four hoofed feet canted upward from the bloated stomach.

One of the more astute male students murmured, almost to himself, "It's, it's a pony." In a more astonished tone, he turned to the rest of the class and said, "It's a freaking pony, like, a little horse."

Another of the less astute students said, "Its dead."

Marla looked at him and said, "Duh, of course it's dead. You think it's sleeping?" She looked at Billy Bob, "So, what's up with the dead pony, you hit it with your car on the way home last night?"

Billy Bob couldn't muster a quick come back so he said, "No, this here pony came from Jimmy Jervis's farm. His kid's growed and got tired of it and he got tired of feedin' it. If you look close here," he leaned over the head and pointed his finger, "you'll see a nice little hole in its head where he sent this guy on its way with," he looked a little closer, "kinda looks like a twenty two."

The room remained quiet, only the humming of the fluorescent lights providing background noise, the students still trying to comprehend the purpose of a dead pony sprawled in front of them.

"This here is what they call a miniature horse, not really a pony. A pony would be about twice this size and weigh five or six hundred pounds. This little fella weighs somewhere around two fifty, but is a good size to give you a feel for the anatomy of livestock. So, a couple of you guys get up here and help me hoist this thing onto the cutting table."

"You gonna cut it up?" One student asked, his chair screeching on the concrete floor as he pushed back away from the carcass.

"Not gonna actually butcher it, just show you some of the pertinent areas of the carcass; so you can recognize the terms used in the industry, like, hind quarter, loin, back strap, stuff like that. Now, give me a hand." Billy Bob grabbed the front two feet and waited for some assistance. None came.

Marla got up. "What a bunch of wimps." She walked up and grabbed two legs. "Let's do it." Holding the two back legs spread apart she said, "Uh, where's his, you know, his…"

"What," Billy Bob said, "His nuts? They cut those off so he'd be calm and not try to hump everything."

"Yeah, that'd do it, alright." She looked at Billy Bob and thought *he'd be a good candidate for that operation as well.*

They slid the carcass off the cart onto the table, the movement causing some intestinal gas from the bloated stomach to escape with a loud hiss. Marla, being on the receiving end jumped back waving her hand. "Jeez, how long's this thing been dead?"

Another student turned white and jumping up headed for the door, unfortunately not making it out of the room before puking in the corner. The smell of vomit permeated the room on top of the raunchy horse fart and suddenly, the other four male students ran for the door, all holding their hands over their mouths.

Marla moved back away from the table but stood her ground. "You still think this was a good idea?"

The horse fart was just another typical slaughterhouse smell to Billy Bob, but the smell of vomit was starting to make the stagnant tequila in his unstable gut do flip flops. He wanted to say something but the pressure against the back of his throat insisted that he not open his mouth.

"Felling a little queasy there big guy, one too many last night?" Marla turned to leave the room. "You guys are all a bunch of pussies. I've smelled worse than that in the girls' high school locker room. Let me know when you want to cut this thing up."

CHAPTER 14

Marla made a beeline for the ladies restroom, located in the back of the building next to the former stockroom, now the day care. Even though she feigned lack of disturbance from the pony incident, her stomach was a little queasy and she needed something to calm her nerves. She pulled a joint from her tool belt and sat down in a stall to relax. After two or three hits, she leaned back and smiled, thinking about the past half hour and the past few months. She couldn't help but laugh out loud just thinking about the whole school thing. This was her second semester and she hadn't looked at a book, hadn't taken a test, hadn't done anything except pound a few nails and strut her stuff on the job site, yet, she was accumulating credits toward some sort of degree. She had read about how college athletes made it through a university for four years and never learned how to read, but figured that was written by some disgruntled teacher or someone that couldn't make the team.

Bottom line, this wasn't such a bad gig after all. Everyone seemed to be happy, including her parents who had suggested there may even be a car in her future if she continued to be such an all-star student.

She heard the door open and close and doused the remains of the joint, feeling much better. Two bare feet walked past her stall as she opened the door. A smallish girl wearing a hair bonnet and long black dress stood at the sink washing her hands. Marla walked up to do the same and said, "How you do'in? If you don't mind me askin', where's your shoes and, what's with the hat thing?"

Mary Good looked up at Marla but didn't speak.

"Is this like some kind of religious thing or something? Like, don't get me wrong, the hat thing is kind of cool, in a way."

"You're not supposed to smoke in the building." Mary went back to washing her hands.

"Well, yeah, like, it's not really smoking, it's medicine. I mean, I have to do it for my nerves."

"You mean, smoke marihuana, for your nerves," Mary said casually as she dried her hands.

"You're not, like, some kind of undercover cop are you? I mean, yeah, I smoke a doobie every once in a while, but it's not like I'm dealing or anything. So, seriously, what's with the outfit, if it's not a costume, why you wearing it?"

Mary sighed, like she had answered the question a thousand times. "My family abides by a fundamentalist form of Mennonite doctrine. Women are forbidden from exhibiting any form of dress or attire that will attract attention."

"Looks to me like you did just the opposite, you stand out like a scare crow in a punkin' patch."

102

Mary looked at Marla, giving her the once over. "Why do you have all those markings and rings? Are you trying to attract attention?"

"No, like, it's style; I'm stylin'."

Mary continued, "But, what if you decide you don't want them anymore, or the style changes?"

Marla had kind of struggled with the question at times herself, but usually just lit another joint. "You think this is going to go out of style? I don't think so. Besides, somebody will probably invent some kind of magic cream that erases all this stuff. I'm not worried. So, you on break between classes or something?"

"I came in here because they are getting ready to take pictures and do some kind of commercial in the daycare and I don't want to be on TV. Remember, the attract attention thing."

Marla perked up. "Pictures of who, commercial for what?"

"I really don't know. There is a whole crowd of people, including Mr. Scales and Mrs. Ringwald. Before I left, they said they wanted something called a live action of the day care. The lady that runs the volley ball team is there too." Mary adjusted her bonnet in the mirror and said with some distain, "She hardly has anything on," and then chuckled, "her teets are sticking out like cow udders before milking."

"Her what?"

"Teets." Mary put her palms under her breasts and pushed up to emphasize her point.

"Oh, tits. Yeah, I know who you're talking about, the hooker from the Falls. She's in the commercial? They must be getting desperate." Marla adjusted her tool belt, opened another

103

button on her blouse, further revealing her newest tattoo and said, "Come on, let's go see what's going on."

Mary hesitated, silent.

Marla stood at the door, holding it open. "Come on, what's the matter? This could be fun."

"I should get back to the daycare."

'Yeah," Marla said indignantly, "and I should be studying for my next exam. What, you think they are going to do, flunk you or something? What's your name anyway? Mines Marla. Some of the guys call me Ringo, or sometimes the slutster."

"I'm Mary, Mary Good."

"Can't argue with the last name, that's for sure, but, you know, a better name for you would be, like, Hats. Seriously, the hat thing is pretty cool. I may even go for one of those myself, different color of course." Marla looked out of the door. "Look, here they come. They're headed for the biology lab. This ought to really be a hoot. Come on Hats."

Marla grabbed Mary's arm and they walked out into the open lounge area of the building and fell in line with the camera crew that was following Scales, Rowena, Chad Overstreet, from the Governor's office and Lisa Calmwater. Her arm was looped through Overstreet's arm and she wore a skimpy halter top, even though it was forty degrees and spitting sleet outside. Numerous students dressed in khakis and dress shirts, an unknown commodity any other day of the year, and Randy Lipinski, dressed in his best blazer and striped tie brought up the rear.

Marla approached Randy from behind and gave him a little pat on the butt. Randy stopped abruptly and turned. "Oh, it's you, Marla. I've asked you before, please don't do that, it could give the wrong impression." Marla blew him a kiss and stuck her tongue ring out through a big smile.

Scales was leading the group, walking backwards, gesturing with his arms as he talked. "We are especially proud of our biology lab. Our anatomy class is one of our premier programs that will soon be part of our practical nurse curriculum. We expect approval from the accreditation committee in the near future. Professor Redbone heads the department, although he is absent at the moment."

Getting closer to the glass enclosure, the lower opaque portion of the wall hid the lower part of the interior of the room, but the upper windows revealed four hooves sticking up in the air.

Scales, still backing toward the room saw the glazed expression on Rowena's face and turned. From his front of the line position he could see the pony sprawled on the stainless table and Billy Bob Redbone lying prone with is arms crossed on his chest on a bed of four chairs in a row at the front of the classroom. Scales abruptly stopped and held up his hands, palms out, halting the approaching entourage. Once the movement stopped and foot clatter arrested, everyone could hear the rhythmic snoring within the glass enclosure.

Marla moseyed up to the glass and rested her arms on the ledge separating the glass from the lower portion of the wall. "Looks like ol' Billy Bob had a rough night, and I'd say that pony didn't do much better."

The rest of the crowd stood on their tip toes looking at the scene in amazement. One of the camera crew said, "Get that thing rolling, I want a picture of that horse. That's what it is, isn't it, a dead horse?"

Overstreet, standing close to Lisa, nonchalantly wrapped his arm around her and whispered in her ear, "What do they do with a dead horse?"

Lisa whispered back, close enough to Overstreet's ear to lip his lobe, "I don't know. I've seen 'em use live ones before, in porn movies, if you know what I mean, but, who knows what Billy Bob's doing."

Scales, jaw hanging open stuplified, was at a loss for words.

Billy Bob snorted, tried to raise his arm to shoo a fly off his nose and promptly fell of his bed of chairs hitting the cement with a splat. He tried to stand, leaning against the table that held the pony, and said to himself, but loud enough for his unknown audience to hear, "God damn it stinks in here." He rubbed his nose with his sleeve and turned to leave and was confronted with twenty some faces, all staring at him through the glass.

Marla smiled and winked at him.

Billy Bob rambled over to the door, swung it open and said, "Anything I can help you folks with?"

Jim Scales grabbed Billy Bob by the throat with both hands and pushed him back into the room and they both tumbled to the floor. Scales repeatedly pounded Billy Bob's head into the floor, the whole time howling like a coyote with his nuts caught in a trap.

The camera kept rolling.

Rowena jumped on Scales back and tried to pull him off Billy Bob yelling, "Don't kill him now, there's too many people watching."

Billy Bob, running out of oxygen due to Scales hands wrapped around his throat, made one last ditch effort to free himself by throwing a round house at Scales but missed and caught Rowena on the end of the nose. The loud crack brought oo's and ah's from the crowd. Rowena slapped her hand over her nose as the blood spurted between her fingers. She pulled her hand away and looked at the blood, spit on the floor, gave Scales a mighty shove rolling him off Billy Bob and promptly started pounding Redbone in the face with her bloody fist yelling, "You miserable piece of crap, you broke my nose," while blood spurted profusely from both their faces.

Billy Bob, starved for oxygen and being pummeled by Rowena, rolled into a ball and covered his head.

Finally, Randy came to the rescue and, keeping good distance so the blood didn't splatter on his Brooks Brothers wool blend slacks, pulled Rowena away from the fray and gave her a roll of paper towels to staunch the bleeding.

Billy Bob, sensing the opportunity to escape, crawled toward the door but lacked speed enough on all fours to avoid Scales who once again jumped on his back and put a hammer lock on his throat.

Lupinski wrestled Scales off Billy Bob's back asking everyone to calm down.

Lisa, realizing this may be the end of the day's activities, rubbed Overstreet's thigh and said, "Would you like to go back to the daycare and see the nap room again? I think I need to lie down after all this ruckus."

Marla turned to Mary and said, "Come on Hats, let's you and me go for a walk, I think the shows over."

CHAPTER 15

All of the combatants and a few other observers some bandaged and still bleeding and others not, sat in a semi circle in Scales office, no one speaking, waiting for the meeting to begin. Rowena had a wad of paper towels smashed against her nose held in place by some adhesive tape. Billy Bob held a big towel filled with ice against the side of his head covering one eye that had swollen shut. Scales sat at the front of the group, his shirt and sport coat splattered with blood; the knot of his silk tie askew with half of the loop around his neck exposed where his shirt was torn; and a wet towel wrapped around his right fist to alleviate the swelling.

The only one with a smile on her face was Lisa Calmwater, adjusting her halter top and humming an unrecognizable tune.

Scales rubbed his forehead with his towel wrapped hand and said, "So, can anyone here explain what just happened? Or, for that matter, can anyone explain why there's a dead horse in the biology lab, because if anyone can, I would sure like to hear it."

No one spoke. The only noticeable noise was Rowena wheezing into her paper towel.

"Okay then, let's start with you, Billy Bob. It's your classroom, and I assume, your horse. That's a start anyway."

Lisa Calmwater spoke up, "Excuse me, may I be excused from this, this, whatever it is? I need to get home and get cleaned up, Chad's picking me up." She made another adjustment to her halter top, starting to stand and sliding her sunglasses that were perched on her head down over her eyes.

"Chad, Chad who, the Governor's guy?" Scales asked. "I figured the whole bunch packed up and left town. He's still here?" He made eye contact with Redbone's one good eye. "I imagine he's pretty unhappy at this point, probably complaining to the Governor right now."

"Well, when I left him, he had a big smile on his face, I can tell you that," she waltzed toward the door, "and I suspect he'll be smiling tonight too."

Rowena said as the door slammed, "How's that for a case of political di-blow-mancy."

Redbone moaned, "Don't do that, God it hurts too much to laugh."

"So, this is all a big joke to you all, huh? Just a big gag; kind of like pin the tail on the dead pony, that it? Well, it's not so funny to me." Scales was starting to shake and spit as he talked. "Do you realize what just happened? Everything I have worked for just blew up in my face."

"What about my face?" Redbone said, dabbing the ice against his eye. "I ought to sue someone. I may have a conclusion."

109

"You mean a concussion? Just shut up Billy Bob," Rowena wheezed under the paper towels, "or I'll give you something worse than a concussion. You broke my nose, you, you dip shit. What were you planning on doing, humping that pony or something? If my husband was here you'd either be dead or in the hospital ICU with a Priest hanging over you."

Redbone leaned back and closed his one good eye.

Scales sighed and leaned back in his leather chair. "Let's hear it, Billy Bob. This may be your one and only chance, so it better be good."

"What," Redbone said like there was nothing to explain. "It's an anatomy class. That's what you do, you cut stuff up. But, before we even got that far along, one of those pussy kids got sick and then the whole bunch of them took off."

"A pony, you were going to cut up a *pony*?" Scales exasperation was rampant. "What happened to frogs, or cats, or even a fucking pig, but a *pony*?" He rubbed his forehead again. "Okay, where'd the pony come from? You kill it with your truck or something, because, if you just went out and killed some kid's pony and it's in my building….."

"I didn't kill the pony, and it ain't a pony anyway. It's a miniature horse. They use 'em in petting zoos and stuff like that. Jimmy Jervis had it for his kid and I guess the kid got tired of it or grow'd up or something. Anyway, he, you know, disposed of it in a humane way," Redbone shaped his hand like a gun and placed it against his head and pulled the trigger. "I saw him at the club, and he's tellin' me about it, and I thought, hell, this would be a great learning tool, you know, explain the intricacies of butcherin', stuff like that."

110

Scales stared at Redbone, trying to calm himself and hoped the pounding in his head was not a precursor of a stroke. He rubbed his forehead for about the tenth time and asked, "At the club, huh. I assume we're not referring to the country club."

"It's the BE club, over in the Falls."

"That would be *Bare Essentials*, would it not? This just gets better all the time. Where's the, the horse or pony, or whatever now?"

"I wheeled it out to my truck. Som bitch is heavy. You wouldn't think so, with those tiny legs. It was starting to stink a little, so I figured on dumping it tonight."

"So Billy Bob, after all these people saw that thing, probably have it on camera, you figure on going out on some back road and dumping it. I got that right?"

Billy Bob gave it a few seconds thought and responded, "Or bury it…."

Scales interrupted, "You freaking moron. That's just what we need now, somebody finding your dead pony laying by the side of the road and thinking, hey, that looks just like the pony that idiot had at the school. We better call PITA or the EPA, or God knows what government organization to figure out why some jerk-off, wise-cracking, laid off butcher threw it in the ditch. That sound about right *Billy Bob*."

Redbone rubbed his head. "I probably have a contussion or something. I'm just not thinking straight."

CHAPTER 16

Marla and Mary took seats near the vending machines, watching the crowd disburse from the lab. Mary, with her hands folded in her lap felt tense because of her absence from the daycare. Marla wished she could flare up another joint as the buzz from the first one was starting to fade.

"What's it like on a farm, I mean, you live on a farm with animals and all that. You have chickens? They're cute. Like, I had a chicken once, one of those colored ones they have at Easter. I kept it in a box in my bedroom. The only bad part was the smell, and the scratching all night. But then Rosco, that's my cat, he ate it, well most of it, he left the feet, didn't like the feet. We went to Smith's dairy farm when I was in, I don't know, like third grade or something. You talk about stink. Half the kids puked in the bus before we even got to look at the cows. You got cows, Hats?"

"We have three milk cows and a couple steers. I should be getting back. Mrs. Cummins will be upset, me being gone so long."

Marla leaned back, relaxing, getting into the conversation. "Don't worry about her. Like, what's she going to do, go recruit some more students to work in her daycare? Believe me, she needs you more than you need her. You got any pigs? You know, I saw on some TV show, Animal Planet, or something, that pigs are one of the smartest animal's there is. You believe that? Can I come to your farm someday? I could dig that. Maybe I can repair something," she adjusted her tool belt.

Joy Cummins marched across the big room with a stride that would have impressed General Patton. "Mary," she commanded, "what are you doing? I've got twelve kids in there crying, half with shitty diapers and the other half puking up their lunch. And you sit out here with this, this…."

"This *what*," Marla said with conviction. "She's taking a break. You don't like it, go find somebody else to do your work. Like, this is a school, not a factory. Matter of fact, maybe we should form a union." Marla got up ready to get in Cummins face.

"I don't have to put up with this. You're a student. You can't talk to me like that. I'll go to Dr. Scales and have you expelled."

Marla smiled, "You might want to check the hospital after that fight in the biology lab."

Mary rose and started for the daycare. She turned and said to Marla, "Thank you, I mean for talking to me. You can come to my house anytime you want."

"Hats, remember, we are students, don't let this old hag boss you around. See you tomorrow."

*

113

Mary and Marla started meeting near the vending machines with regularity as their friendship blossomed. The dichotomy of their appearance while sitting side by side became a topic of muted conversation by the other students.

Spending time with Hats had tempered Marla's wardrobe to the degree she no longer exposed her cleavage tattoo and had started wearing long, although extremely tight, pants. The tool belt still hung conspicuously on her hips.

Mary had taken on new, less conservative appearance as well, much to Mr. Good's consternation, donning black dresses that exposed her ankles and wearing running shoes with bright fluorescent coloring, but only after she arrived at the school and accessed her personal locker in the daycare.

Rico Clemenza and Johnny Rotton maneuvered their way through the lounging students, Rico pushing where a simple "excuse me" would have sufficed, and Johnny following up with a laugh or a muffled comment.

Clemenza wore a leather jacket with the sleeves cut at the shoulders; chains hanging like ammunition belts; blue jeans so dirty they appeared to be dyed black and black boots with metal buckles. Rotton tried to emulate Clemenza but failed miserably; his jacket appearing to weigh him down and his jeans recently washed, probably by an attentive mother, rolled up at the ankles to expose his new boots.

Clemenza sauntered up to the vending machine closest to Marla and leaned against it, picking at his teeth with a toothpick held between two dirty fingers. "What's happenin' Slutster? Who's your new friend? Been to a church meetin' or something?"

Johnny Rotton stood slightly behind Clemenza, hands on his hips, trying to take on the same aura of toughness without success. "Yeh Slutster, who's your buddy, and what's with the bonnet? She looks like a nun or somethin'."

Marla slowly turned her head and sized up the duo and said, "Shut up Johnny." She then turned her attention to Rico. "What are you doin' here Clem? The entry level might be pretty low here, but at least you have to graduate from high school."

"We was just checkin' the place out," Rico replied. "I like your tool belt, where'd you get it?"

Johnny snorted and said, "Yeah, where'd ya get it?"

Rico said without turning his head, "Shut up Rotten."

Mary couldn't help but stare at the two in disbelief or at least astonishment.

Marla exhaled expressing her exhaustion with the interruption. "Why don't you guys go steal some hubcaps or something and leave us alone."

"Oh, the high and mighty college student doesn't want to associate with us, huh Rotten. Since when's the Slutster got so good, huh Rotten?"

Marla slowly turned her head to face Rico. "You got nothing better to do, Rico, than stand around and act like some kind of gangster? And by the way, It ain't working."

"Fuck you, Slutster. You ain't no better than us, and we both know that. Ain't that right Rotten."

The profanity made Marla jump to her feet and standing on her toes, put her face to face with Rico. "Don't ever use that language in front of me and my friend again, you understand, Rico?"

Rico turned his head and spit out the toothpick.

Marla repeated slowly, *"Do you understand?"*

Rico gave a slight smirk. "Or what?"

Marla brought her knee up hard into Rico's groin, and she later swore she heard a squish, like a water balloon hitting the floor.

Rico let out a giant burst of air and went straight to his knees, curling up and groaning, cupping his scrotum through his dirty jeans.

Johnny Rotten stood looking down at Rico and said, "Jeez, Marla, why'd ya have to go and do that."

Mary said, *"Ouch,* I bet that hurt."

Rico whispered, "I think I'm gonna puke."

CHAPTER 17

Father Carolle Cardone, ruling Priest of the Hinkley Catholic Barromeo relaxed in his *Barco* lounger, feet elevated and arms hanging loosely over the pillow topped arm rests. His three hundred plus pound body seemed to be absorbed into the chair; his chin hiding his reversed collar and his rhythmic inhale/exhale consistently separated by a high pitched snort, the only sound in the room. His Italian heritage had endowed him with rich black hair that even at the age of sixty had not begun to recede, though years of cigar smoke had produced deep worry lines aging his round face.

The daily nap Father Cardone was enjoying followed his traditional lunch of sliced salami, olives, warm bread, modest salad of spring greens and a large bowl of linguini smothered with the sauce of the day. His napkin still clung to his chest with splotches of red sauce still visible and his lunch tray, pushed to the side of the chair, revealed his appetite had not wavered.

Mildred Tanner, the Parish office secretary and cathedral organist was instructed to allow a minimum of two hours of solitude after lunch, officially known as a time of prayer and self evaluation. Following the time of prayer, the Priest would hear confession on a first come, first serve basis until the evening mass at five o'clock.

The two hour allotted time for solitude had elapsed and Mildred silently entered the library next to Father Cardone's office where he napped. She picked up the lunch tray and took it to the dumb waiter hidden in the book shelf that would transport the dishes to the basement kitchen.

Father Cardone snorted, rubbed his nose and apparently lapsed back into slumber, mumbling between snorts, "snnnnn, don't, don't, snnnnn, (chuckle), oh yeah baby, snnnnn, (chuckle), ooh, ooh, ah, snnnn, (chuckle)......" He opened one eye to see if Mildred was listening.

Mildred, used to the musings of the fat Priest after fifteen years serving as his personal secretary, nurse maid, valet and consultant with regard to female counseling, was not impressed. "If you are having that much fun, maybe you should skip confession today and just nap through the afternoon."

Father Cardone reached down and flipped the lever dropping his legs to the floor and raising the back of the chair to a sitting position. "I thought I had you going there for a minute." He yawned, started to scratch his belly and realized the napkin was still there and removed it. "Do we have any customers in the confessional?"

"Please don't call them customers. We've had this discussion before. Someday, someone is going to overhear your ill placed humor and then what will you do?"

"Now, Mildred my dear, a little levity never hurt anyone. You didn't answer my question, anyone waiting down stairs?" Cardone eased himself out of the recliner with a rolling motion that brought him to a standing position. He straightened his suspendered pants, tucking in his shirt and looked toward the hall tree where his black suit jacket hung, a signal for Mildred to retrieve it and assist him.

"Rowena Ringwald is down there, the only one as far as I know." Mildred threaded Cardone's arms into the jacket, picked up a lint brush and brushed the shoulders and back, turned him toward her and tugged at the sleeves, licked her palm and patted a protruding misplaced strand of hair and then stepped back, giving a final examination before turning and walking toward the doorway. "She's ringing her hands, so it must be some sort of personal problem."

"What ever happened to the good old days when you got the typical confession; I slapped Johnny too hard; I spent the household food money at the casino; a little adultery now and then? Now it's some sort of emotional problem that would take Sigmund Freud to figure out." He glanced at his watch. "Oh well, let's get it over with."

The confessional consisted of a telephone booth like compartment in an alcove of the chapel. Father Cardone entered an adjoining booth from an opposing door; the assumed sinner separated by a wood panel with a small sliding door allowing communication without face to face confrontation.

Cardone slid the little door open, crossed his arms and leaned back against the wall of the booth resting his arms on the girth of his stomach. There was no sound. He waited about

119

a minute and still there was no sound. He coughed, thinking maybe Rowena didn't realize he was there, still no sound. He leaned down and looked through the rectangular hole provided by the sliding door and saw Rowena's hands clasped on her lap and said, "You awake?"

"Okay," Rowena said blowing out a big breath like she was preparing for a fast ball in the bottom of the ninth with men on base. "Bless me Father for I have sinned. It's been....." She paused trying to calculate the last time she had been to confession. "Well, it's been a long time. Actually, I can't remember the last time."

Cardone closed his eyes, resting his head on the wall and said, "Uh huh, there's the first one, sin I mean."

The part that really made this difficult for Rowena was that she knew Cardone like a brother, not a father. They went to school together, lived down the street from one another, played together at the park on warm evenings, and even experimented with some kissing and petting at one time in their early teens. He was known as Cardy and she Row and they made a pretty good friendly couple until he went off to college and at some point decided he needed to spend three years at a monastery without speaking and then enter the seminary bound for Priesthood. Not that Rowena felt she was slighted in any way by his absence in her life, she was happily married, but revealing her personal issues to Cardy was difficult, to say the least.

"Well, since the last time, whenever that was....."

"Let's just say it was a long time ago, my child, and get on with it."

"Jeez, Cardy, are you this short with everyone? Give me a break, I'm trying to remember."

"Alright, Row, I'm sorry. We'll stick to the script. Tell me your sins my child, since your last confession, whenever that was."

"Well, there's probably a long list of little things, I mean, like swearing and stuff like that."

"Oooookay, that's pretty normal, and what else?" Cardone thought, *here's where it gets sticky, especially if this has something to do with infidelity or some other indiscretion that is probably already common knowledge all over town.*

"Well, I'm not sure where to start."

Cardone discreetly glanced at his watch. *This could be a long one,* he thought.

"You know I work at the community college, don't you?"

"Yes, my child, go on." Names of the men working at the school flashed through Cardone's mind anticipating Row's admission of some nefarious act.

"And it's been going pretty good, something like a hundred and fifty kids in the second semester. I mean, I get paid good, and really don't have to do anything, other than keep track of the admissions and fill out some of the loan applications, especially for the kids that can't write too good, or read for that matter."

"And the sin part, my child. I seem to remember something about bless me for I have sinned."

"Okay, I'm getting to it. Just keep your pants on Cardy. Well, here's the thing, I guess my conscious is bothering me some. I mean, we take all this money from these kids, or the kids parents mostly, or the government….., *for what*? Supposedly they are getting an education, or getting trained for a job of some sort, but mostly, they are working for the school, building houses or potty training infants. Need your car fixed? Send it over, we've got twenty kids working in our body shop."

Rowena abruptly stopped confessing and there was silence.

Cardone leaned forward and said, "That's it?"

"What do you mean, that's it? I could go on. Did you hear about the horse in the biology lab?"

Cardone rubbed his chin. "You didn't steal anything?"

"Cardy, what, you think I'm a thief?"

"I didn't say that"

"Sure sounded like it." Rowena sniffed and rubbed a tear from her eye.

Cardone, used to the tell tale signs of an impending wale said, "Row, I don't know that the confessional is the right place for this discussion. So, how about we finish up here and go to my study. In mean time, bow your head and cross yourself. You will repeat four Hail Mary Mother of God as penance. God the Father of mercies has sent the Holy Spirit among us for the forgiveness of our sins. May God give you pardon and peace and I absolve you of your past sins, including not coming to mass for I don't know how long, in the name of the Father and the Son and the Holy Spirit. Now let's go upstairs and have a cup of coffee."

*

Mildred brought the tray of coffee and some cookies to the study. "High Rowena, how's Jerry? Sure miss him in the choir. He used to belt out those low notes like a big tuba."

"I'll tell him you asked. I guess he got tired of the regiment, and then there's practice on Thursday night, right when the football game comes on."

Mildred busied herself straightening some of the bookshelves and checking the waste basket.

"Thank you Mildred," Cardone said as a manner of dismissal.

Mildred, not one to be dismissed, made a couple more adjustments to the shelves and scooted the desk chair in a little. She looked at her watch and said, "I must get ready for the Knights of Columbus Ladies Auxiliary meeting tonight. Nice to see you Rowena. I'll be in the office Father, if you need me."

They both watched Mildred leave the study and close the door with authority.

"And they wonder why Priest's don't marry. Now then," Father Cardone began in a relaxed tone, "what about this school thing. I've heard such good things about the school, or college, or whatever it is. Why Jennifer Rodriguez said her son is getting straight A's. He's in some sort of cooking class. A little strange, he likes to cook, but I suppose there are a lot of good jobs in the restaurant industry."

"Yeah, that's the Art of Creative Cooking class. He'll get a certificate of completion and a guarantee that Max at the Kountry Kitchen will hire him to wash dishes when he graduates."

"Whoa, you sound a little cynical there Row. If the kid wants to learn how to cook, what's the problem with that?" Cardone picked through the cookies until he found one to his liking.

123

"I don't know Cardy, it just don't seem right sometimes. Okay, the creative cooking class has a textbook, which is really a cookbook you can get anywhere, and after they read about a recipe, they go into the make shift kitchen that has two used stoves, a refrigerator and a couple mixers and they cook something. That's assuming the girls from the day care aren't in there mixing formula or something. And here's the kicker, Scales has this idea of actually putting in a professional kitchen and then running a catering service using the students as the cooks. You get the picture? Use the students to build houses for the big shot board members; use the students to fix their cars; use the students to run a day care, that by the way, netted almost eighty thousand in the last six months. Where does it stop? And the government is promoting it for God's sake. Sorry, or is that allowed, I don't remember."

"See, if you came to mass you would know. By the way, where did Jim Scales go to get his doctorate? I don't recall him getting an undergraduate degree, at least while I was in school."

"Probably *Kinko's*, or the internet."

"That's funny. No, really, what school?"

"You're kidding, right? It's not funny, it's pathetic. He didn't go to school. He was lucky to graduate from high school. It's what he calls an honorarium. He anointed himself, get it?" Rowena gave a frustrated sigh.

Cardone chuckled. "Seriously, he goes around calling himself a doctor and he didn't even go to a college. That takes some brass balls." Rowena gave him a stern look. "Yeah, I'm allowed to say that, it's in the father knows best book."

"You'll never change, Cardy." Rowena started to get up.

"Wait a minute," Cardone said, "You came here for a reason, and so far, I haven't heard it, other than you are disappointed in the way Jim Scales is conducting himself. Excuse me, Doctor Jim Scales. So, what advice are you looking for? I mean, if you don't like the way things are going there, quit."

Rowena sat back down. "Okay, so I quit, nothing changes, they still run the money mill and what happens to the kids? The parents are happy because they think their kids are getting educated; the politicians are happy because they can say they are supporting education; the so called professors are happy because instead of having to work for a living, they have the students do it. Everyone's happy, until they get the delinquent student loan collection notices, or the *sorry, there isn't any job for someone with a certificate of excellence in diaper changing.* What then?" She stared at Cardone, waiting for a response.

"Good question, and one that should be asked. Probably not to me, but by some authority that regulates this type of institution. Isn't there a school board or something?"

"Cardy, haven't you been listening? This is a for profit school. No one cares except those that are raking in the money. For profit means the more kids we get through the door the more money we make." Rowena shook her head, "I'm not looking for answers here, I guess I just needed somebody to listen for a few minutes, that's all. You did your job and I appreciate it. My husband gets tired of me griping about it all the time."

Cardone stood and took Rowena in his arms and hugged her tightly. "We go way back Row, and I know what's in your heart, it's the kids. Let me think about this for a while. I might even go over there and take a look. You show me around? That would be nice."

"Anytime Cardy, you know that."

"See you at mass Sunday?"

"Thanks again Padre;" Rowena smiled and headed for the door, "maybe."

CHAPTER 18

Randall Lupinski sat at his desk leafing through a periodical, Admissions Weekly, directed toward college admission directors divulging the latest tactics on how to build student population without really trying. He had just closed his two hundredth new student for the fall term, and the high school graduation season was only beginning. It was like bringing the spring sheep to slaughter, when you thought about it. Ninety percent of the kids get their diploma and are in a complete fog, have no direction, no job, no future. And then Randy, the savior, shows up at their doorstep offering continuing education and a place to hang out at their parent's expense, just like high school never ended. Shazam, they sign the contract and Randy deposits another five hundred bucks.

Next to the periodicals on his desk lay the latest brochure displaying the new model year for BMW. He had already picked out the model he intended to lease at just shy of one thousand a month. Two student contracts would be all it took to cover the new expense.

Jim Scales threw open Lupinski's office door and entered without knocking, followed by a short guy dressed in a navy blue blazer with his shirt collar spilling over the lapels. His pants looked like they had been balled up in a grocery sack prior to being stretched onto his legs and they crumpled over his well used wing tips. He wore black framed glasses hanging on a pointy nose and had receding thin hair giving him a Mr. Peepers first impression. But then, on closer inspection, his beady black eyes and a mouth that turned slightly upward, something between a snarl and a smile, gave a more sinister greeting.

"Randy, meet Phil Overholt. Phil, this is Randy Lupinski, our director of admissions and recently, heading up our business school. Randy, Phil's going to take over recruiting, isn't that right Phil? He has loads of experience. Comes from Genoa Junior College over in Danford, was the top recruiter there for how many years, Phil?"

Phil's turned up smirk didn't change and his lips hardly moved when he replied. "'Bout ten years, not all recruiting though, did some other stuff for the school too."

Scales interrupted Phil's response. "This is prime recruiting season and seeing how you are tied up with the business school startup, I wanted to give you some help meeting that five hundred student goal for the fall semester. I've already expanded the search area another fifty miles at the call center and that should generate another three or four hundred leads. Just keep track of your mileage Phil and I'll reimburse you.

Mileage, Randy thought and almost blurted out, *you never gave me any mileage expense.*

Alright then, I'll let you two get acquainted. Randy, be sure you give Phil that call center appointment list so he can get started first thing tomorrow. Remember guys, five hundred is the magic number." Scales turned and headed for the door. "By the way Randy, try to have that new business math course study ready for me Monday so I can get it to the printer and in the fall semester menu of classes." Scales closed the door and Randy could hear him whistling as he headed back to his office.

The words *take over recruiting* kept banging around in Randy's head. He had just settled into the lifestyle of the rich and famous and Scales was yanking the rug out.

"This where you sell the paper?" Phil asked. "Bring 'em in here and wow 'em with your credentials. Nice touch." He wondered over to Randy's degree plaque from Marquette hanging on the wall. "I got one from IU, bought it on the internet, little better quality than this. Where'd you get yours? Can get you a better one if you want, you might think about using some other school though, these country kids probably never heard of Marquette."

Randy's ears were burning and his voice was catching as he tried to respond. "*I didn't buy anything.* I earned that diploma, as well as most of my graduate work at Notre Dame."

"Well, excuuuuse me," Phil said with a chuckle. "Then why aren't you professerin' at some big school instead of in this hick town, in what, *a converted grocery store?*" Phil slowly turned from inspecting the plaque and said through the turned up smirk, "Could it be the easy money? Naw, a guy like you, on the high ground, with all the degrees, you wouldn't stoop to selling diplomas, would you?"

"It's not selling diplomas, it's......."

"Hey, you don't have to justify what you do for a living to me. I've been in this game long enough to know exactly what we're doing, and it ain't educating today's youth; babysitting, maybe; running a social club, even closer; but it ain't educating, I can tell you that." Phil slouched down in the chair facing Randy's desk. "Look, I'm not trying to be a hard ass here, you be whatever you want to be and believe whatever you want to believe. All I can tell you is that by August, I'll have this place full of hop heads and deadbeats and any other kid that is able and old enough to sign a promissory note, and if he ain't, I'll get his low life parents to sign." Phil pulled a pack of Winston's from his jacket pocket and started to stick one in his mouth.

"You can't smoke in here or anyplace on the campus," Randy instructed.

"Yeah, right, you tell those two kids smokin' the joint out front that?"

The office door jarred open and Billy Bob Redbone stuck his head in. "Phil, you ready to go? Man, I got a thirst like you wouldn't believe."

Phil smiled, "Billy Bob here's gonna show me around, take me to his club. Ain't that right Billy Bob? What's it called?"

"What, the club? It's *Bare Essentials*," Billy Bob responded. "You been there, haven't you Randy?"

Lupinski was still wallowing in the desperation of the rug being pulled out from under him with regard to the recruiting commissions and was barely paying attention to the conversation. "Where, what club, the country club?"

Overholt's eyes brightened. "You belong to a country Club? Man, the pickin' must be better 'n what I thought. Which club? They got golf and everything?"

"No, no, I don't belong to the country club. Dr. Scales does, and we've had some meetings there."

Billy Bob interjected, "Not the country club, the strip club. The one Lisa owns, or partly owns, you know, over in the Falls." Billy Bob looked at Overholt. "Lisa's our athletic director and teaches a massage therapy class. Wait 'til you see her. She used to do a pole dance that could make a limp dish rag stiff. Now she pretty much stays in the background, seein' how she's pretty high up in the school and all. I think Scales is thinkin' about makin' her a doctor too."

Lupinski rubbed his forehead in exasperation. "No, I haven't been to the *club*. But from what I hear, Billy Bob is a steady customer."

"Nothing wrong with that," Phil said with a smile. "Sounds like my kind of place and you need to introduce me to Lisa." Phil crooked his neck until there was a loud crack. "I could use a good massage."

Phil rose from his chair. "Get me that call center list first thing in the morning. I'll be ready to make appointments tomorrow, assuming Billy Bob doesn't get me in some kind of trouble tonight."

CHAPTER 19

Marla Todd cruised down the Good farm lane in a ten year old Chevrolet that bottomed out on every bump and trailed blue smoke that rose in a feint cloud over the tree line that stretched along the fence protecting the drive. She slowed to a stop a few hundred feet from the house letting a row of chickens peck their way across the drive and sat admiring the scenic view of the farm.

A tall red barn graced a neatly trimmed lawn with a fenced pasture behind rising to a tree line. Four black steers stood watching her, their snorts pushing out steaming air swirling around their massive heads. A spotted black and white dog with a knob for a tail eased its way off the porch and cautiously moved toward her car. It didn't bark or growl, but rather stopped every few feet and raised its head sniffing, as though it was trying to identify the intruder.

Marla let up on the brake and eased a few more feet and the dog started prancing alongside the car, trying to get a glimpse of the occupant. The gravel drive gave way to grass and Marla stopped and parked, continuing to admire the picturesque setting. The expansive porch held rocking chairs, a swing, several empty flower boxes that she imagined would be full of blooms as the winter gave way to spring, and an American flag slanting out from a post lightly furling in the breeze.

A figure appeared behind the screened door, like the dog, trying to identify the trespasser. Marla stepped out of the car and was immediately involved in a licking contest with the speckled dog. He jumped from side to side, tongue out, stub tail wagging, and then would run up and lick Marla's hands and face when she bent down to pat it on the head. She was so enthralled by the dog's reception, she didn't notice Mary stepping off the porch and approaching.

Looking up, Marla said, "High Hats, like my new car? Isn't she cute?" Marla wore a hoody, jeans, work boots and of course, her tool belt.

Mary smiled, bent down and gave the dog a pat. "Stay down Sam. He gets all excited when we have company. I didn't know you had a car. It is cute, I guess, for a car."

"My parents gave it to me. They said it's because I'm doing so good in school. Wow, what a neat place. I can't believe you have animals, like, everywhere. Don't the cows just, like, wander away or something? And the chickens, don't they just fly away?" Marla bent down and Sam washed her face with his leathery tongue.

A big cat came around the house and slowly made its way to the gathering. Sam growled when he saw it, but Mary scolded him. "Sam, leave Peanut alone." She looked up at Marla, "He thinks this is his yard and Peanut is just here because he lets her."

Peanut ignored Sam and did figure eights around Marla's legs, swishing her tail like a big fan.

"You want to come in," Mary said, glancing at the front door. "My parents went to town for groceries. They go every Saturday afternoon."

"Sure, like, what are you doing, I mean, have you fed the animals yet?" They started walking toward the house, Sam and Peanut following. "What do the cows eat?"

Mary stopped and took a hard look at Marla. "You look different. The rings are gone."

Marla had a nose ring, tongue ring, three piercings on each ear, and those were just the visible decorations.

"Yeah, like, I kind of grew out of that. You know what I mean."

Mary's vague expression gave a good clue that she didn't know what it meant. "You had so many, and now you have none."

"Can we see some animals? You have any in the house? I saw this, like, show on TV, about some people way off somewhere, and they kept pigs in their house. Yuk, like, can you imagine....?" Marla stopped and thought for a second. "Like, you don't have any pigs in there do you? I mean, if you do, it's alright. I didn't mean, like, you know, there's anything wrong with that."

Mary laughed. "We don't have any animals in the house, well, except Peanut, and Sam sometimes, when he finds a way to sneak in."

Mary showed Marla around the house, through the kitchen, up the stairs to her bedroom, decorated with handmade dolls and crocheted blankets.

"It's so clean," Marla marveled. "Everything is spotless. You have, like, a maid or something?"

Once again Mary was a little wary of the question. "Why would you ask that?"

"Someone has to clean this place. I've never seen a house this clean. Don't you ever throw your clothes on the floor, or lay on your bed?"

"I sleep in the bed, if that's what you mean. And then I make the bed when I get up."

Peanut came prancing into the room, jumped on the bed and sat there staring at Marla.

"She's waiting for you to pay attention to her," Mary said.

Marla went to the bed to pet Peanut and sat down beside her. She quickly jumped up attempting to straighten the wrinkles in the bed spread. "Sorry, I'm not used to this."

"Let's go downstairs. Would you like something to drink?"

Marla pictured a Budweiser long neck or maybe a Leinie's. "Okay, like, what you have?"

"There's some lemonade. We have milk, but you may not want to drink it because we don't pasteurize, it's straight off the hoof. Some people are afraid of it."

Marla scrunched her face. "It's what, pastured, what's that mean, like, they don't deliver it in a truck or something?"

As they walked to the kitchen Marla explained the story of Louis Pasteur and how milk is processed for retail sale.

Marla said, "Hats, like, you are the smartest person I have ever met. You know, seriously, you shouldn't be at that stupid school. You should be at a real university, IU or something like that. I wish I was as smart as you."

135

"You are as smart as me, probably smarter. You've experienced so much more than I, and you have so many friends."

Marla shook her head. "Yeah, like Clem and Johnny Rotten at school? Who needs enemies when you have friends like *that*."

Mary continued, "I have been thinking about the school, and what you said. They do seem to be using me, us, without much in return. I can't blame my parents, they don't understand. They just think a college is a college, no matter what goes on, as long as I get some sort of diploma."

"Yeah, mine are the same way. I hear my mom all the time on the phone, *Our Marla is getting straight A's, can you believe it.* But, like, it got me a car. You want to go for a ride?"

Mary smiled, "I can't leave while my parents are in town." She looked over Marla's shoulder and said, "There they are now. You'll get to meet them."

Ralph Good climbed out of the pickup truck and took a long look at the strange vehicle parked in front of the house. Then turned and made the same exhaustive inspection of the house before starting a firm stride toward the porch. Mary and Marla stepped through the screen door to greet him.

"Father," Mary greeted, "this is Marla Todd, my friend from school I told you about."

Ralph, not one to smile or express any emotion, looked at Marla like a drill sergeant inspecting recruits, and didn't comment.

"Marla, this is my father, Ralph Good, and my mother Audrey is in the car." Audrey hadn't moved, apparently waiting for Ralph to signal she could get out.

Ralph turned and looked at Audrey and she began exiting the pickup and carrying grocery bags toward the rear door of the house without acknowledging Marla. Ralph still stood silent.

Marla, confused by the awkward introduction said, "Okay then, nice to meet you Ralph. You need any help with the groceries? How about we feed some animals, like, anything around here you want fixed?" She adjusted her tool belt and smiled.

Ralph remained expressionless with exception of the worry lines in his chiseled face seeming to grow tighter.

Sam, sitting next to Mary, seemed a little confused as well, waiting for an opportunity to play if someone would just throw a stick, bobbing his head in one direction then another.

Ralph said, "Mary, your mother will need help with dinner."

Mary responded with some strength in her voice that seemed to startle Ralph. "I would like to show Marla around, take her to the barn to see Mariah," she glanced at Marla, "that's my horse." She turned back to Ralph, "I think mother can handle dinner this once."

Ralph stared at Mary for quite a spell, their eyes meeting like lasers before he turned and walked toward the house, ignoring the open truck door and remaining grocery bags.

"Is he always that happy?" Marla asked sarcastically watching Ralph enter the house. "He needs to chill out, like, he's gonna have a coronary or something. Where's the animals?"

Mary led the way to the barn as Ralph watched through the parted curtains in the kitchen. "I told you this would happen," he snapped. "The elders warned me, women aren't supposed to be let loose to go their own way." He rambled as though he was talking to the neighbor over a fence rather than to his wife in the same room. "They don't know right from wrong; follow anyone that comes along. I should have listened, but I thought, well I thought Mary was different, thought she could do it."

Audrey said meekly, "She's just a friend from school, it's good she has a friend."

"By God woman," Ralph responded harshly still staring out the window, "can't you see what's going on here. Didn't you see those tight pants, the way she draws up her chest? She's a harlot, the devil. I could see that the moment she stepped from the porch. Who knows what she will do next. We could have a gang camping out in our orchard. I've got to put a stop to this."

"Please, Ralph, we'll talk to Mary after her friend leaves."

Ralph slowly turned to Audrey. "Don't tell me what or when to do anything, woman." He slowly walked into the next room.

*

Mary and Marla strolled leisurely through the barn, followed by two adolescent kittens, tumbling and attaching each other in faux play as they tried to keep up. The smell of hay, horse manure, machinery oil and the earthen floor, mixed to enliven Marla's inquisitive spirit.

"Dude, look at the size of that thing," Marla said pointing at the palomino mare standing in a stall, hind quarter facing them.

"That's Mariah, my best friend, well my best animal friend next to Sam. She's fifteen years old, I've had her almost my whole life."

Mariah turned her head almost as on cue, giving a snort and then turned in her stall to face them. She lifted and lowered her head like she was approving the inspection.

Mary pulled an apple from her apron and presented it over the stall gate. Mariah's big lips parted and she inhaled the red ball in one colossal chomp. After she swallowed she shook her head and whinnied with pleasure.

Mary smiled and caressed her nose.

Marla cautiously approached the stall. "Does he bite?"

"It's a she, and no, she doesn't bite, well, she's not fond of my father and has nipped him a couple times, but most of the time she's gentle."

"I can understand that," Marla said moving closer. "Can I touch him, I mean her?"

"Just rub her snout, she loves that. And if she parts her lips, don't be frightened, that's just her way of letting you know she likes you."

Marla drew closer and slowly closed the distance between her outstretched fingers and Mariah's nose. Mariah raised her head and placed her nose within reach and scrunched her lips like she was preparing for a kiss. Marla touched the skin between the horse's nostrils and rubbed.

"It's, like, it's, it feels like velvet. It's so soft." Marla could feel the horse's exhales in her face and marveled at the new experience. She turned to express her feelings to Mary and to her surprise, Mary held a kitten in her arms, caressing its head. "He's so cute," Marla said reaching for the kitten.

CHAPTER 20

P hil Overholt pointed his cue stick at the corner pocket and said, "Eight ball in the corner off the bank." He chalked the cue and bent over the table drawing a bead. With a light tap the white ball bounced off the rail and bumped the eight ball into the pocket. He stood, a smirk of satisfaction displayed as he turned to his opponent. "I'll take that beer, make it a Bud."

The defeated kid, dressed in a tee shirt with the short sleeves trimmed to the shoulders and dirty blue jeans with a fat silver chain draped like a loose belt, moped over to the bar as instructed. He brought back the cold beer and slammed it down on the side of the table. "Fuck'in lucky shot. Fuck'in couldn't do it again if you fuck'in wanted to."

Overholt smiled, "You're probably right. I'll tell you what, let's up the ante some."

"The fuck'in *what?*"

"What we play for, you know, the bet." Overholt took a swig of the beer and looked at the bottle. "Man that's good. Here's my proposal."

The kid slouched down on a stool. "Just fuck'in tell me what we are fuck'in betting, okay?"

Overholt rubbed his chin. "I'll tell you what, how about we bet your future? If you win, I sign you up for the next semester at the community college, no charge. If I win, let's see, we'll sign you up but you have to sign some extra papers saying if the school gets you a job, you'll pay some of the money back. Chances are, that's not gonna happen, so it's a win win for you."

"Fuck'in *school*? I'm not going back to no fuck'in school. Jeez, you fuck'in nuts or somethin'?"

Overholt smiled and put his hand on the kid's shoulder. "Nobody said anything about going to school. It's not like high school, it's more like a club. You go hang out with your friends, drink a few beers, play some pool; maybe even get on the Hinkley Hooters pool team and play other college teams."

"They got fuck'in pool tables, *at the school*?"

The hook set, Overholt picked up his cue stick. "I'll even let you break."

CHAPTER 21

J im Scales sat at the Hinkley Country Club bar looking at the lone olive in the bottom of his empty martini glass. The bar tender worked her way down the bar in his direction.

"Get you another Mr. Scales?"

Scales looked up and forced a smile. "Yeah, and save the olive."

"Will the other gentlemen be joining you this afternoon?" She asked with her back to him while she prepared his drink.

"Uh, I'm not sure." Having expected the question, Scales folded a fifty dollar bill and slid it across the bar holding it under his hand until his drink was delivered. The martini was placed in front of him and he removed his hand. "Just in case Mrs. Scales calls......."

The fifty was nonchalantly slipped into a fold of her apron. "And where shall we say we are, just in case Mrs. Scales calls?"

"The usual, somewhere out on the course, or down in the private card room."

"And, if Mrs. Scales arrives in person?"

Scales took a sip of his martini and winked. "Son of a gun, I just left, probably passed on the highway."

*

The wealth generated by the college came so quick and in such volume, Jim Scales was overwhelmed with the new prosperity. It seemed like he couldn't spend the money fast enough. If he invested in the school, the reward seemed to be three or four times the amount in return and kept growing. He installed a new row of vending machines, investing twenty thousand dollars, rather than leasing or sharing the profit with the former vendor, and the return had doubled in the first six months. The child care center was generating clear profit of ten thousand a month, not including the tuition collected from the forced labor. The new recruiter was putting students on the books faster than the loan papers could be filed.

Scales ran every expense he encountered through the school and took a two hundred and fifty thousand dollar salary on top. He decorated his new home at the school's expense; installed his new pool; leased two Cadillacs; bought his daughter a condo in Florida representing it as a recruiting office; bought Lisa Calmwater a Caribbean Cruise for certain considerations not in her employment contract; and the list went on and on.

The only personnel aware of all the ins and outs of the money trail was Rowena, and her salary had climbed to just shy of one hundred thousand, and took a bump every time she mentioned any guilt or reflection on the actual purpose of the school.

143

Scales primary administrative function had been whittled down to trying to hide profits or at least keep expenses in line with the profits.

John White, the school's banker referred Scales to his Chicago accountant and tax consultant to offer suggestions and find ways to make the school's tax return so complicated that the Harvard Business School would have to devote half their Rhodes scholars to interpret.

All of the tension and stress related to the operation of the school left Scales with realities he had never anticipated. He had just maneuvered through his fifty fourth birthday and while enjoying the entrepreneurial challenge of operating the new school and the related rewards, he faced a mid-life crisis as he reviewed his personal accomplishments and predicaments. His marriage had turned into rare face to face encounters that generally degraded into unwinnable arguments. Sexual encounters were out of the question, at least with his wife. Living in Hinkley was like living in a fishbowl, one couldn't walk out on the porch to retrieve a newspaper without ten people having knowledge and questioning motive.

Throughout Jim Scales's adolescent and adult life he had suffered from an inability to approach or communicate his feelings to women. His wife had literally taken his hand at a post high school party and led him into a bedroom to consummate their relationship. Having been the only woman to ever show interest, he married her.

He used his awkward social skills in his management positions at the gas station and the grocery store to hold

144

himself above reproach when it came to women employees and any flirtation thrown his way. He would always say he rebuffed any advances because of his high moral standards when really it was his weak knees and dry mouth that stifled the foreplay.

Lisa Calmwater, well skilled in the remedies necessary to instill confidence in the meekest male, noticed Scales troublesome problem along with his restless demeanor and decided to intervene. She invited Scales to her club, *Bare Essentials*, to experience what it was like to be released from his self conscience inhibitions.

Being introduced to strippers and uninhibited ladies of the night was a new beginning for Scales. After his initial indoctrination at *Bare Essentials*, he realized that a strip club in Cougar Falls must be at the low end of the food chain and given his new monetary stature, progressed to traveling to larger city venues and patronizing the escort services offered clandestinely in high class hotels. He would schedule a business meeting in Chicago or Louisville, and after becoming a familiar customer, have an escort waiting for him in his reserved suite.

Few knew of his new found pleasures, but like every conquering male, little bits of information would slip either on the golf course or after too many martinis. Rumors passed, but no firm condemnation had arisen. So, his business travels came on a more frequent schedule and attention to detail at the school diminished.

*

Rowena Ringwald, one of the few who figured out what was happening, could not hold her distaste and cornered Scales in his office, knocking and opening the door without an invitation. "Jim, I know this is none of my business, and you know I have always respected your personal activities and privacy, be what they may, but Jim…, hanging out at Calmwater's club, like some, some, *like Billy Bob Redbone*? Is that what you want to be compared to? I can picture the headlines, *Dr. Scales caught in the middle of a lap dance when strip club gets raided*. Is that what you want?"

Scales looked at Rowena like she had her wig on backwards. "What? Who said anything about Calmwater's club? Okay, I went there a couple times because she wanted to show me some decorating she did, but…… Who said I spend time there? You been talking to my wife?"

"No, there's just some talk going around. You know how it is, someone sees you there and the next thing you're a regular customer. Don't forget what happened to the school superintendent. He practically got tarred and feathered when he got caught there. What was her name, the one he got caught with, Barbara Boobalicious? I'm just saying, it's not good business. You want to do that kind of stuff, do it someplace where no one knows you."

This brought a smile to Scales and he subdued the laugh. "I haven't been to that club for I don't know how long. You know me Rowena, that's not my style. If I was out looking, you know your door would be the first one I would knock on."

"And you would be met at the door by my husband."

Scales did laugh this time. "Okay, let's just drop this. I got your message and I know it's just your way of showing how much you care."

Rowena continued her hard stare trying to define the truth from fiction. She couldn't. Scales façade held strong and finally she turned and returned to her office.

The conversation aroused Scales so much that he dialed the Drake Hotel on Michigan Avenue in Chicago on his cell to make a reservation. Once completed, he pulled a small black note pad from his locking desk drawer and phoned an answering service.

"How may I direct your call?"

"Cinderella."

"And whom may I say is calling?"

"Pinocchio."

"I will advise Cinderella of your inquiry." The phone disconnected.

Scales breathed heavily and sweat beaded on his brow. The anticipation of the return call was almost too much to handle. There had been times when he sat for hours staring at the phone awaiting the return call. He had never been disappointed. Five minutes passed and the cell phone chirped. The dial signal said restricted.

Scales opened the line but didn't offer a greeting. After all, he was the submissive part of the act, taking, not giving direction.

"Pinocchio, how good of you to call. Do you miss me?"

Scales could hear himself breathing into the phone and tried to calm down. "Yeah, I miss you a lot. Uh, I hope you miss me too, I mean, miss getting together, that part."

"Oh Pinocchio, you are so cute. You make me laugh. Did you just call to make me laugh?"

"Uh, no, I have to be in Chicago tomorrow, and, you know, will you have time.... to see me?"

147

"Oh Pinocchio, I am so busy tomorrow, I don't know. I would have to cancel some plans. But, if you make it worthwhile, I can try to adjust, just for you."

Scales tried to hold his breath to keep from hyperventilating. "Oh, I'll make it worthwhile."

"It would have to be double, Pinocchio, since I am changing all my plans."

"Whatever….., the same time?"

"Yes, Pinocchio, the same time, everything is the same." The phone disconnected.

A shiver followed his placement of the phone in his pocket. He stared at the blank wall in anticipation of what was to follow the next day. Then the realization hit that he had not scheduled any trip, either with the school or his wife. First he called Rowena. "Uh, I just got a call from the, the, the governor's office, yeah, and they want me there tomorrow, well not actually there, but in Chicago…., for a meeting."

"A meeting, for *what*, or what kind of meeting?" Rowena was not an easy sell.

"It's some kind of, I don't know, some kind of educational forum, it's part of that stuff the governor's pushing, you know, every kid learns to read, something like that."

Rowena didn't respond immediately, and then said, "Jim, don't bullshit me, okay. What's going on? Does this have something to do with our conversation a few minutes ago? Don't answer, because if it does I don't want to know. When are you coming back?"

"Probably the next day, but I'm not sure, so keep my calendar clear."

"Jim, I don't have a calendar. I'm lucky I have a clock. So, what you are saying is I am supposed to lie for you until you decide to come home."

Scales gave a snort to display his fake distaste for the comment. "Just make it work, and I'll bring you back a calendar."

His next call was to his wife.

"Janet, honey, I have to go out of town tomorrow. Just found out."

"*What*," Janet Scales blurted, "out of town where? What about the dinner party at the club with the Whites? That's tomorrow night. Just cancel your trip." With that instruction, she hung up.

Scales dialed the number again. "Honey, I can't cancel this meeting, it's with the governor, I mean, not personally, but at his request."

There was silence with exception of the heavy breathing that sounded like a bull moose was holding the phone. "Where's the meeting?"

Her monotone not lost on Scales, he tread lightly. "It's in Chicago," he said slowly, his mind churning out facts as fast as he could develop them, "at the Hiatt, kind of an educational forum, something like that."

"Something like that, huh? Does this something like that include wives?" (inhale…exhale)

(Churn, churn, churn) "Well, this is kind of informal, not a dinner or anything like that, that you would enjoy, I mean, mostly just a bull session, with other educators."

"Bull being the key word, right?" The monotone was gone. "I'll tell you what, I'll just come along, Doctor Jim, and you and I can shoot the bull, how does that sound?"

149

Scales began to lose patience with the conversation. "Well, *hon*, I don't think that will work, me being the only one there with a wife. So, why don't you call the Whites and re-schedule; I'm sure they won't mind."

(Inhale, exhale, click)

CHAPTER 22

Father Cardone walked through the front entrance of the Hinkley Community College and marveled at the facility. After only a year, the grocery store had been converted into a relatively handsome institution of learning. Students milled around the large selection of vending machines, some sitting at tables reading, others playing pool or foosball. Especially impressive were the two girls sitting together toward the back of the big open room, one dressed as one would expect for an adolescent, except for the tool belt, and the other obviously Mennonite or some similar sect that demanded a strict dress code.

Rowena Ringwald caught his eye stepping out of the hallway leading to the administrative offices and they walked toward each other. Rowena greeted Cardone, "Father, so glad you could make it, you hit it about right. All of the classes are letting out and you get a good feel for the atmosphere, assuming you can stand the swearing and tainted smell of marihuana."

CRAIG SULLIVAN

Cardy looked around the room and smiled. "It doesn't look too bad to me, they're just kids, like any other school." He sniffed, "I don't smell anything offensive."

"Want a cup of coffee or a Coke? We have the latest vending technology available. A caterer from the Falls comes in every morning and stocks pre-packaged sandwiches, soups, deserts, you name it, it's there. Dr. Scales tried to get the culinary classes to do that stuff, but it was a little over their head. After all, tuna salad takes some imagination, and a few brain cells."

"Come on Row, you're being a little hard on them, aren't you. Could you make tuna salad in high school? Okay, don't answer that, and don't call Jim Scales doctor. That about makes me sick."

"Is that any way for a Priest to talk? Anyway, these vending machines turn a tidy profit each month."

They continued to slowly walk through the bustling crowd of students.

"Those two are an interesting couple," Cardy said directing Rowena with his eyes to Marla and Mary sitting together on a bench at the end of the vending machines. "What's with the tool belt? Is that some kind of fashion statement?"

"That's Marla Todd, one of our more colorful attendees. She specializes in tattoos and piercings, although for some reason they are not as noticeable today. The tool belt just goes with the territory. The other one, I'm not sure about."

Father Cardone directed their slow walk toward the two girls and said, "Introduce me."

Rowena gave a questionable glance but moved through the crowd ending in front of Marla and Mary. "Ladies, this is Father Cardone, he asked to meet you."

152

Mary shot out of her seat and stood before Cardone with her hands clenched looking at the floor. Marla didn't move other than to cross her legs and adjust her tool belt.

Father Cardone placed a hand on Mary's shoulder, "Sit down my child, no need to be so formal. I just wanted to meet you and tell you how nice it is to see two young ladies challenging their intellectual abilities."

Marla said, "Challenging *what*? What's with the collar? I kind of like it."

Rowena sternly said, "He is a Priest, Marla, show a little respect."

"That's alright," Cardone said, "I kind of like your tool belt. You getting ready to build something?"

Rowena rolled her eyes and sighed.

"I might," Marla replied, "depends on which of the big shots around here wants a new house. After all, that's what we're here for, isn't it?"

Cardone seemed to miss the insinuation or at least ignored it and he looked at Mary. "And what about you, do you have a specialization or course of study?"

Mary looked up and said, "I work in the day care."

"So, you're not a student."

Marla gave a snort. "Yeah, like, we're all students; students of how to make the owners rich. The trouble is, Mary here actually thought she was going to get an education."

Mary said, "Mar, please."

Rowena clutched Cardy's arm. "Thank you ladies, we'll leave you alone now."

Cardone said, "But, I don't ……"

Rowena pulled him away.

Cardone asked as they walked away, "So, is that what's bothering you?"

Rowena hesitated and then responded, "Well, in some ways, I guess it is. Like today, Dr…, Jim Scales is off chasing tail in Chicago someplace while kids like Mary are working in the day care. Yeah, sometimes it bothers me. How many of these kids know when they get done playing pool and volleyball they have to pay some shylock loan company payments for the rest of their lives? I doubt if any of them do."

"I see what you mean," he said scanning the room once again. "What do you mean Scales is off chasing tail?"

"Just forget I said that," Rowena said turning to return to her office.

"Seriously," Cardone continued talking to Rowena's back, "where is he, I'd like to talk to him. He have some kind of issue, I mean, with women?"

Rowena didn't respond until she closed the door of her office. "Look, this is just between you and me, okay."

"Row, I'm a Priest, remember."

Rowena sat down and fidgeted with her hands on the desk and exhaled deeply. "Jim and his wife have been having some problems. So, then I find out Jim is spending time at Lisa Calmwater's strip club."

"Who's Lisa Calmwater?"

Rowena hesitated, "She's our athletic director and teaches message therapy."

"Ohhhhkay, and runs a strip club on the side. That's interesting."

Rowena rubbed her forehead and continued. "See, I've known Jim Scales for a long time, and he's no ladies man, not by a long shot. He's got more inhibitions than a deer on the opening day of gun season. Anyway, apparently, the strip club just didn't do it for him so he started using call girls or escort services when he's out of town. At first it was just an occasional trip and it blended in with his expense account. But then the trips started getting more frequent, like two or three times a month without any legitimate reason, you know, like a conference for college presidents or something. How I found out, well actually my husband found out was when one of Jim's golfing buddies had too much beer and started talking about how Jim would spend a grand in one night on a hooker. I mean, I didn't believe it, but then I started looking at his credit card bills and how much cash advance he was taking each time he left town and put two and two together. Now, it's almost once a week."

Cardone pulled at this collar and said, "I guess it's his money, mind you, I don't condone what he's doing, but he's not the first."

Rowena threw up her hands. "Cardy, that's all you've got to say, he's not the first? Well, I guess that says it all. Why should I care about these kids and the fact the owner of this ATM machine is spending thousands of their dollars on hookers when my priest says, *Hey, it's just a guy thing.*"

"Row, I didn't say that. I said he's not the first wayward soul that sought refuge through ladies of ill repute. I had a brother in the priesthood," Cardone crossed himself and looked toward the heavens, "God rest his soul, who lost his way and resorted to fouling his vows in the same way. It doesn't mean he is beyond salvation, it's a cry for help."

"Yeah, well I'd say he's screaming, or somebody's screaming about now."

Cardone ignored the comment. "The question is, what are we to do?"

"About what?" Rowena asked.

"About your concerns; about the kids that are getting shafted out of an education; about Jim Scales slide into iniquity. What are we going to do?"

"How does this sound, I'm going to go home and have a beer with my husband. You're welcome to join us."

"Row, I know you better than that. This has been eating at your gut for quite some time or you would not have come to me. Now I'm part of it, so we're in this together. There has to be some answer or way to turn this around, for everyone's benefit. So, go get your husband and come to mass at five, and by then I may have some answers. Anyway, we can pray on it and that will certainly help."

Rowena stood, "You go give mass and pray that I don't get fired for spreading rumors. In the mean time I'll have that beer and we'll talk again soon, assuming the prayer thing works."

CHAPTER 23

Marla and Mary watched Father Cardone and Rowena walk away.

Mary said, "I wish you wouldn't say things like that. I don't want to cause trouble."

"Truth hurts, hon. Like I've told you before, I'll never get out of this dumpy town, but you… you have everything it takes, and it ain't right…."

"Isn't…. right," Mary corrected.

"Yeah, whatever. Somebody's got to tell it like it is. If that fat Priest wants to know the truth, then I'm the one to tell him." Marla adjusted her tool belt like she was getting her six shooter ready for a showdown. "Anyway, old lady Ringwald's right there with the rest of them. We'll probably be building her house next."

Mary bowed her head. "We shouldn't talk about a man of God like that. He's a Priest and I'm sure he is sincere."

"See, that's what I mean, you think of stuff like that. While I'm thinking about what butt cheek to get tattooed next, you're thinking about the good things in people and what you can do for them. You know, you would make a good Priest. Isn't that what they do, talk to people and try to bring out the good? Hey, you'd be Mother Good, that's perfect."

"First of all, Priests are men. The Catholic equivalent for a woman is a Nun. I would be Sister Good.

Marla slapped Mary on the knee, "That's even better, Hats. Yeah, Sister Good Hats."

Mary produced an unusual smile.

Marla reached over and hugged Mary. "I'm so glad I met you."

Mary asked, "You're not getting another tattoo…, on your butt, *are you?*"

*

Mary returned to the day care center and Marla had time to think about the visit by Father Cardone. *Maybe Hats was right, maybe he is sincere and wants to help straighten the place out.* She decided to have a talk with Rowena Ringwald, just to clear the air.

Marla approached Rowena's office door that was cracked open and raised her hand to knock but heard her conversing on the phone and settled back against the wall to wait for her to hang up.

"……… He's on another trip, I think he said Chicago……… Yeah, it's almost every week now, and it's always the Drake, I saw his credit card bill………. No, I'm the one that pays it, he won't let the accountant see it…………. What do you mean, how do I know he's with a hooker, is it normal to go to a luxury hotel and spend twelve hundred bucks in the bar, *in one night*? Besides, you're the one told me Ralph told you he was doing high dollar hookers……….. Cardy says it's like a sickness. Oh, and he wants us to come to mass tonight……….. Yeah, I already told him………. Okay babe, chili sounds fine, with a cold Leinie's, can't beat that…… love you too."

Marla thought, *whoa, twelve hundred dollar hookers!* She decided to forego the confrontation with Ringwald and went outside to smoke a joint and give this new information some thought.

CHAPTER 24

Randy Lupinslki sat in his office and watched a cockroach climb the wall and scurry behind his *Pepsi, the pause that refreshes* illuminated clock. Over the past few months his income had dropped substantially due to his newly assigned duties teaching and administering the business school curriculum. The fact that Phil Overholt mined the leads list before he ever got a look kept his hit ratio for new recruits so low he was having trouble making his car payments. He made a mental note to have a stern talk with Scales; no he would threaten him by saying he was going to quit; maybe tell him he would go to work for another school; or better yet, go to the Accreditation Board with the numerous complaints he had stuffed in his bottom desk drawer.

The complaints were starting to be a problem. Some of the early recruits, those that signed and after the first semester, never attended classes or simply disappeared from the attendance sheet, were now getting collection letters and threatening phone calls to their parents residences from the lending institutions, suggesting credit would be harmed or free money distributed through filing of a tax return would be garnished if the deadbeat student didn't begin making timely payments.

Lupinski had been cornered twice by bearded, tattoo laden past students who made rather frightening threats that included castration, broken bones and simple outright beating. Fortunately, each event ended with only the verbal threat, and some unsightly underwear stains.

The bottom line, when all things were considered, he was ready to take this job and shove it. Then he would look at his latest American Express credit card statement along with the tab he had run up at *Bare Essentials,* his new method of escape, and reconsider. Rather than walk away from what had once been a cash cow, he needed to develop a plan of action to get back in the saddle. He had already approached Scales about the competitive edge given to Overholt when it came to recruiting, but the complaint was received with less than enthusiastic response. Scales seemed to be off in another world, finding it difficult to absorb even the most basic observation, such as his steadily declining income. Scales just blew him off and said he needed to make more appointments and sell more tuition. And while they had their frank discussion, Scales was constantly checking his cell phone for messages and when he did look up, Lupinski got the impression Scales wondered why he was still there.

The next lower rung on the ladder was Rowena Ringwald, so Lupinski strolled down the hallway and knocked on her door. Rowena stood behind her desk, "I'm just leaving, can it wait until tomorrow?"

161

Lupinski stepped in anyway. "High Rowena, getting ready to leave," Lupinski looked at his watch. "It's only three."

Rowena plopped down in her chair. "Dr. Scales is out of town, so I'm leaving a little early. Something you need?"

"Out of town again, huh," Lupinski sat down in front of her desk. "He seems to be on the road a lot lately. Anything I should know about? I mean. We're not going to be under new ownership or anything, are we? I'd hate to be left out of the loop, if you know what I mean."

"No, I don't know what you mean." Rowena picked up her purse and put it on her lap and leaned forward, giving an apparent hint that the conversation was ending.

"He just seems a little distracted lately, I mean, I talked to him about some concerns I have and he just, well he just didn't seem to comprehend how important it is to me. You know what I mean?"

"No, I don't know what you mean." Rowena pulled her car keys from her purse and held them in her hand, jingling.

"Where did he go?"

The question was so blunt that it caught Rowena off guard. "He's in Chicago at the Drake..... *What difference does it make where he is*? I really don't think...."

"No, you're right, it's none of my business, but you have to admit, he's been acting kind of loopy lately."

"*Loopy, w*hat's loopy mean? That some fancy word you learned in college?" Rowena dropped her keys back in her purse, realizing Lupinski wasn't taking the hint.

"You know, *distracted.* I mean, okay, here's an example; I tried to talk to him about all these complaints I'm getting from

162

disgruntled parents and the threats I'm getting from some of the drop outs that aren't happy about their loans.... You know what he told me, sign up some more kids. That's his answer to everything. And Overholt, he's a piece of work and a whole other story. He's putting kids on the books that don't even know their enrolled. I saw one kid's application; you know the part where it asks what high school you graduated from, he wrote unavailable, in other words, the kid never graduated, probably dropped out. And now he has a student loan and is supposedly taking classes.

"Tell me Rowena, is that the way this is supposed to work? Just get them in the door and get their money, or their parent's money, or the government's money, which is usually the case. Is that what this is all about?"

Rowena sank back in her chair. "How many complaints?"

"Quite a few, and it's not going to get any better. We're only into our second year, so all the kids that got tired of playing pool or baby sitting or fixing cars last year are going to start getting hate letters from the collection agencies this year. Or they will get a legit job or get married and want to get a loan to buy a car or a house, and oops, you've got crap credit because you never paid your student loan.

"And then I heard from one of my counterparts at the IU branch in the Falls, that the Accreditation Committee is launching an investigation..... Apparently, they've received quite a few letters as well. There have even been some words thrown around like.... fraud; money laundering; and I don't know what else."

Rowena's stomach flipped and she squirmed in her seat. "I, I wouldn't know anything about that. Who said *that*?"

"I'm not saying you are involved….., at least in any of that stuff, I'm just asking, is anyone paying attention? There's a whole bunch of money flowing through here, and I'm sure not seeing any of it."

Rowena gave Randy the squint eye. "So, *that's* what this is about; you're not getting your share?"

Randy tried to look offended. "Of course not, I mean, sure, I'm a little miffed about the fact my income has been cut in half and I've essentially been put in charge of what little educational product this place puts out, the business classes, but overall, I'm thinking I better get out before the whole thing caves in."

Rowena sighed, "Yeah, I've had the same thoughts, I mean, not so much about the fraud stuff, that's new to me, but I am concerned about the kids, the students, and the long term effects." She rubbed her forehead. "You know, right now, I'd just like to go home and have a beer with my husband and think about this."

"To tell you the truth, right now I can't afford a beer. So while Dr. Scales is soaking up a twenty dollar martini in the bar at the Drake, I'm eating a buy one get one free burger at Ralphie's. Think about *that* while you are having your beer." Randy got up and walked through the doorway, turning and saying, "Sorry I bothered you Rowena, enjoy your evening."

Rowena sat staring at the empty doorway and thought, *Damn it, I knew this was going to happen.*

CHAPTER 25

Richie Lizardo sat at the end captain's chair in the Coq D'or cocktail lounge of the Drake hotel. He sipped a soda water and lime, biding his time, watching the curved archway entrance through the mirror behind the bar. He had dogged so many cheating husbands over the years that the repetition of the methods they used overpowered any enthusiasm for the chase. Scales wife had gladly paid the retainer some weeks before and after the first set of pictures, showing the pair meeting in advance of their retreat to a private room, had asked for more; she wanted them caught in the act. So, he had received the call from the wife advising of the meeting in Chicago at the Hiatt; knew from past experience that meant the Drake; had his counterpart geek hack the reservation service of the hotel; boosted the assigned room and installed a camera hidden in a tissue box across from the king size bed; and now sat back and counted the billable hours at two hundred per.

Like clockwork, Jim Scales walked into the cocktail lounge, dressed casually with an open collar shirt and sport coat, coordinated slacks and loafers. Lizardo could hear some of the banter between the customer and the barkeep, typical meaningless bar talk. Soon a martini glass appeared and the barkeep strained the chilled liquid into the glass topping it off with a pierced olive and walked away.

The cocktail hour crowd had not gathered, so the room was relatively quiet as Scales sipped his martini, occasionally looking at his watch and turning to look at the entrance alcove.

Scales ordered a second martini, giving the entrance greater attention as each minute passed. Upon reaching the twenty minute mark, he drew out his phone and started pressing numbers. As if he had pressed the code for instant call girl, the same girl Lizardo had seen before stepped into the room. She was tall, smartly dressed in all black with stilettos; brunette hair hanging straight; a little over made up for Lizardo's taste, but still very attractive with high cheek bones and long slender neck. She made her way across the room and took the seat next to Scales. They acknowledged each other but made no personal contact. Scales summoned the barkeep and ordered. Drinks were consumed and Scales discreetly slid an electronic room key in front of the lady and she exited the room. After ten minutes, Scales placed a single bill on the bar and exited as well.

The barkeep worked his way down to Lizardo and smiled while he cleaned the bar top. "She's working her magic again; has him in here once, maybe twice a week now. I don't know what he does, but it must pay a lot to afford her. You know him, Richie?"

"No, never met the guy."

*

"I've got what you wanted," Lizardo said to Janet Scales. "You want stills or the action version?"

Janet exhausted breath into the phone. "What kind of action?"

"'Bout anything you can think of, and maybe some you haven't"

"Jesus, Mary and Joseph, that rotten scumbag. If it wasn't for the children, I'd have it shown at the theater in three D."

Lizardo chuckled, "No doubt, it'd draw a crowd. Anyway, I think my work is done, so I can drop this off and pick up my check. I've got a total of forty three hundred and sixty seven dollars, including expenses.

"No, I want to know when they are meeting again and where."

Lizardo's suspicions perked, "Now Mrs. Scales, this isn't worth going to prison for, no matter how upset you are, and I don't want no part of a set up."

"Why would I go to prison? He's the one ought to be in prison."

Lizardo sighed, "First, there's no law against cheating on your wife, but there is a law against killing your husband, *or his lover,* and for that, they *will* send you to prison."

"Who said anything about killing anyone? I just want to see his face when I catch him with his pants down. And while they are down I want to shove the divorce papers where the sun doesn't shine. So just find out what's next and let me know; then I'll give you a check, his check, out of his account."

Lizardo could hear her talking to herself as she hung up the phone and thought, *it's always the same, they never give up.*

167

CHAPTER 26

Marla and Mary sat in the hay mow of the big barn looking down at the stalls and the farm implements scattered in the big open area. Marla wore coveralls over a t-shirt complemented by her tool belt with Converse lace-up basketball shoes. Mary held her knees to her chest, dressed as usual, hair net, long dress and plaid blouse buttoned at the neck line.

Marla stopped chewing on a piece of straw and pulled it from her mouth. "This sure is peaceful, like, it's just too neat; the smell and the sounds. I can't believe I've missed this my whole life."

"You are only nineteen, it's not like you don't have time to enjoy it," Mary said with a smile.

"I know, but you know how much time I've wasted, screwing around with a bunch of losers; acting like some kind of hoodlum? I know this sounds, like, mushy, but since I've met you, well, I feel like I've changed, I mean, I don't want to start going to church or anything."

Mary looked at Marla, "Mar, I've changed too. That's what friendship is all about, it's about learning from each other. You know things I've never experienced and that helps me understand, well understand me, if you know what I mean."

"You think I can be as smart as you someday?"

Mary didn't answer, just smiled.

Marla continued, "It sure isn't going to happen at that crappy school."

Mary said, "Probably true."

"You should try to get out and go to IU or one of the real schools. You could get a teaching degree or something like that. You'd be a great teacher."

Mary leaned back and stared at the hewn beams above. "I know, but there's no way my father will let me go away to school. He doesn't believe in it. He's already getting grief from the church elders. They think since I'm going to the community college, their girls will want to do the same."

Marla turned to Mary, leaning back with her head supported in her hand, fussing with some straw, "If you had the chance, would you go?"

"You mean against my father's wishes?"

"Well, maybe, but I bet you could make him understand. I bet deep down inside, he wants you to be more than, well, a baby sitter."

Mary thought for a moment and then responded. "You don't understand, my parents and their parents before have struggled to maintain an existence separate from the rest of the world. The primary way you do that is by teaching your children to maintain those traditions. If they were to let me go away to

169

school, well, there's a good chance I would stray from those traditions. Education enlightens and enlightenment expands your horizons."

Marla said, "Okay, forget all of that for a minute. What if I said I think I know how to get you a scholarship to IU, like, all expenses paid, would you be interested?"

Mary gave an inquisitive look, assuming the question to be rhetorical. "I suppose, if I had something like that, I suppose I couldn't refuse, but that's never going to happen. And besides, I wouldn't go away someplace like that without *you.*" She gave Marla's arm a shove playfully, smiling.

"I'm serious," Marla said sternly, sitting up. "I think there's a way to get Dr. Scales to understand that you need to be someplace where you can get a legitimate degree. You deserve that."

Realizing Marla was serious, Mary took on the same serious tone. "What do you mean, you know a way, Mar?"

"Well, I've been thinking, if we knew something about Scales, like, something he didn't want anyone else to know, he might, you know, be...... well, let's just say, like, willing to help..., willing to pay, or give a scholarship." Marla's eyes darted away from Mary and she acted like she was searching for another piece of straw for a chew stick.

Marla said, maintaining her stern demeanor, "First, that's extortion. Do you know what extortion is, Marla?" She didn't wait for an answer. "That's when you extort money from someone through a threat; it could be bodily harm or any other method, but, *it's illegal.* That means you can go to jail, Mar..... Now, what is it that you know, or think you know?"

170

"Jeez, like, you sound like my mother. Okay, I heard something about Scales, not like a rumor, but like the truth......"

Mary sighed and leaned back again, not really wanting to hear what Marla had to reveal. "So, what is it?"

"Well, like, he's going to expensive hotels and......, do you know what a hooker is?"

Mary slapped herself in the forehead in frustration. "Of course I know what a hooker is or does. Who told you this?"

"Rowena Ringwald, well, she didn't really tell me, I heard her talking on the phone to, like her husband, or somebody like that. Anyway, she's telling this person that Scales is spending a thousand dollars a night on hookers in Chicago. Can you imagine, a grand to get...., well, you know what I mean."

Mary looked hard at Marla. "Don't get any ideas about that."

"I know, I wouldn't do that, but a grand just for laying on your back, it's hard to imagine."

Mary said, "So, you thought you could somehow get to Dr. Scales and threaten to expose his, let's call it, extracurricular activities."

"Well, yeah, kind of. I thought I would go to him and suggest how much you want to go to college at a real university, maybe suggest a scholarship, something like that, and then drop the bomb. Not, like, threaten him, but just give him something to think about."

"What about you, you don't want to go to college? What if he thought it would just be easier just to get rid of you? Ever thought of that?"

171

Marla looked perplexed. "Well, I guess I didn't, but he wouldn't do something like that, would he?"

"Okay," Mary said, "that's enough of this. Mar, just forget about it. It's a bad idea, it's illegal and it's dangerous. I can't believe you even thought about it."

Marla spit her piece of straw out. "I still think it's a good idea. When are we going to feed the ducks?"

CHAPTER 27

J ohn White sat behind his mahogany desk in his office at the First State Bank of Hinkley leafing through the *Wall Street Journal* without reading, pondering what corrective measures he could take to fix his severe hooking tendency when he used his driver. *Maybe a lesson or two,* he thought noticing the red light blinking on his intercom.

"Yes, what is it?" He asked impatiently, having requested isolation from any customer interruptions.

"I'm sorry, I know you didn't want to be disturbed, but Endicott Strom called and wants you to call him as soon as possible; said it's rather important."

Strom, Strom and Strom, Certified Public Accountants with offices on the fifty third floor of the Willis Tower in Chicago, handled all tax and financial matters for the First State Bank and regularly invited White to play golf at their exclusive country club to discuss business. White, assuming Endicott Strom was calling to set up a game dialed his private cell and returned the call.

"Cott, Andrea said you called; sorry, I was tied up in a meeting. You thinking you can get in my pocket again? That last round was just a fluke; I want you to know that."

Strom laughed, "You made it up with your bar tab. No, this isn't about golf, a little more serious, you still on the board of the community college there?"

"Well, yeah, why do you ask, not paying their bill or something?"

"No, that's not the problem," Strom replied in a serious tone. "I'm just giving you a heads up; you might think about resigning or giving some excuse to get some distance."

"*What,* I can't do that; they won't have my house finished until the end of the next semester."

"House, what's you building a house have to do with the school?" Strom asked, perplexed.

White thought about the implications of his answer and was cautious. "Well, the project, or one of the projects for the carpentry class is building a house, you know, hands on, that kind of stuff. So...., as a community service, kind of, the bank puts the money up and then the house gets sold when it's done."

"So," Strom asked slowly, "It just happens that they are building a house that appeals to you, or maybe follows the plans you gave them in advance; something like that?"

White hesitated and then said, "Yeah, something like that."

"That kind of fits in with all the other stuff I'm seeing. Look, you know I favor the client when it comes to manipulating expenses and such, but this place takes the prize. There is so much money flowing through there, I can't find enough holes to fill. Then I find out through the Governor's office that your

174

President is shacking up with call girls, commonly known as hookers around here, for a grand a night."

White rubbed his forehead and looked around the room, like he thought there may be hidden ears. "Why would the Governor have that kind of information, *and tell you.*"

"It wasn't the Governor, his assistant is a member of the Athletic Club down stairs and he's been bragging about this babe he met during a commercial shoot at your school. In between talking about her bra size and the things she does to him in bed, he says she tells him about the rumors floating around about the Pres' and his habit of buying hookers. So, you put that tidbit in the hat with all the other shenanigans that seem to be going on, and it's just a matter of time until the house of cards tumbles down…., probably not a good metaphor given your current construction project."

White responded callously, "Yeah, thanks for the afterthought."

"I'm just sending a warning shot over the bow. You do what you want, but this could end up with some sort of investigation by who knows who, and you don't want to be in the middle of it."

After a moment of silence White said, "I should have known Scales couldn't handle this. He was nothing but a store clerk until this school idea found him. You hand an idiot a pile of money and all sanity goes out the window."

"Store clerk, I thought he had some sort of doctorate."

White chuckled, "Yeah, off the internet; doctor of mixology; or better yet, master of sex education. He never stepped foot in a college classroom, until he built his own."

*

John White sipped his gin and tonic and Collin MacGregor stared at his beer, both occupying a round booth in the back of the Hinkley Country Club lounge.

"That's all I know," White reported. "Cot said things look really dicey, and he should know, he's their accountant."

"You might know," MacGregor said twisting his beer bottle like it was a wet dish towel, "just when they are supposed to start my house. The old lady's gonna have a shit hemorrhage. She's spent the last three months picking out flooring and all sorts of expensive decorations. I tell her the deals off, hard to tell what she'll do."

"Quit worrying about the damn house," White scolded. "I'm worried about a bunch of Fed's coming in here and starting some kind of investigation."

"Easy for you to say, your house is almost done." MacGregor thought for a minute. "You think he's really paying a grand for a hooker? He could go to the Falls and get the same thing for a fifty dollar bill."

"Come on, Collin, I think there's a difference between picking up some hump in the alley and a call girl in a swanky hotel in Chicago."

MacGregor studied the beer bottle label. "Yeah, you're probably right. You ever done that, paid a hooker a grand?"

"I've never paid a hooker period. My life is complicated enough without trying to explain to Cheryl why I got sores all over my privates."

MacGregor blurted out, "Yeah, me neither," and waved at the bar tender for another beer.

White changed the subject. "Anyway, I think I'm going to tell Scales I have to resign from the board. I'll tell him there's a conflict of interest with the bank, or something like that."

"Damn, can't this wait until they at least start my house? I mean, this investigation stuff doesn't just happen all of a sudden. I've seen it on TV; sometimes they screw around for years before they arrest anybody."

White looked at MacGregor like he had just won the stupidest statement award. "So, you are suggesting we wait until they come with the handcuffs, then think about getting out."

"You act like we done something wrong. I don't know about you, but I haven't done nothing. So what, I'm on some board; we don't even have meetings. How am I supposed to know what he's up to?"

"Earth to Collin, what do you think a board is for; oversight. We are supposed to be overseeing what he is doing. It's guilt by lack of doing anything."

MacGregor twisted his bottle some more like he was hoping an answer would pop out if he kept squeezing. "I heard that this sex thing is a disease. You ever hear that? Like the golfer, or some of those basketball guys. They can't play or swing their club unless they scored the night before. Then they get caught and all of a sudden they have to go to some clinic where they get therapy or whatever. They come out and they're like Father Flannigan, never to touch strange again...... Maybe that's what Scales needs."

White gave MacGregor another blank stare. "You think it's a disease? You think buying hookers is a disease? Man, Collin, some of the stuff you come up with; it's entertaining, I'll say that."

177

"So, mister know everything, what are we gonna do? I'm for getting Scales some place and kicking the snot out of him until he straightens up. He's screwing with our lives here. If I end up having to pay someone to build that house, well, it could get ugly. I already bought the lot from that shyster Spinetti. You know, he wouldn't even cut me a break on the taxes. I wanted him to report half and I'd give him the cash for the rest, but no, he wouldn't even do that."

"I told you what I'm going to do; I'm getting out. I can live without the five bills he sends me for the quarterly meeting we never have and I can get the rest of my house finished on my own." White drained his glass and slid out of the booth. "You do what you want. You want to go knock some sense into him, that's up to you, just leave me out of it."

"Hey," MacGregor pleaded, "we're in this together. You talked me into this, this board crap. I never wanted to be a secretary, or treasurer, or whatever I am." MacGregor thought for a minute. "He sends you five hundred? He only sends me two fifty."

CHAPTER 28

The entire faculty of the school milled around the central student union area in preparation of the pre-semester evening meeting, waiting for Dr. Scales to appear and give a rousing Hinkley Hooter speech to kick things off.

Rowena, constantly checking her watch, stood next to Randy Lupinski in the corner of the large room anticipating Scales entrance. "Where is he? Pretty soon they are going to get tired of drinking punch and leave. It was better when we had these at the country club, at least you could get a beer."

"Maybe he's off chasing that, whatever again," Lupinski said scanning the room again.

"No, he's here, I saw him before I came down, in his office, he was on the phone. Now, he may have been talking to *whomever,* that I don't know. Have you seen him lately?"

"No, I've been at my parents and then took some time back at my old apartment, staying with friends, why?"

Rowena started to answer but was interrupted by Dr. Scales running into the room from the hallway wearing a Hooters ball

179

cap and Hinkley Hooters tee shirt, bounding up to the podium. To Lupinski, he looked like he had lost twenty pounds and aged twenty years.

Lupinski said, "What happened to him, he sick or something? He looks like he hasn't slept for two weeks."

Scales shouted over the crowd noise, "*Helllllooo Hooters.* Are you all ready for another great semester?" The crowd settled but didn't respond with much enthusiasm. Scales continued, "And great doesn't give it justice, friends. This semester is going to be monumental, and I mean monumental. Not only are we now offering an associate's degree recognized by the Accreditation Board, but we are embarking on a whole new online curriculum that will allow students from anywhere in the country to attend and become Hinkley Hooters." Scales twisted his ball cap reversing it on his head. "It's rally cap time folks. You are part of one of the fastest growing schools in the country. If you haven't looked lately, go to www.hinkleycc.com and take a look. A student will never have to leave the couch in their parent's living room. Punch that credit card number in and they are off to the races, or better yet, a degree."

Lupinski elbowed Rowena, "When did this happen, he never told me."

"All I know is he said it's all outsourced to some company overseas."

Scales continued to shout into the microphone. "Lisa, Lisa Calmwater, come on up here and give us a cheer. I want to hear that Hooter spirit."

Lisa Calmwater jumped onto the raised podium platform wearing skin tight leather short shorts, halter top with see

180

through camisole and knockoff Jimmy Choo high heels. She raised her hands above her head, bounced a couple times and started clapping and chanting, "Hoot, hoot, hooters. Hoot, hoot, hooters."

Rowena said, "Oh my God," as the crown joined in clapping and chanting.

When Lisa had the crowd thoroughly involved Scales interrupted and continued to rant and rave about the great things happening at the school until sweat beaded on his forehead and discolored his tee shirt. Finally he raised his fists above his head and said, "Praise the Lord and good night." With that, he bounded off the platform and ran for the hallway, exiting just as he had arrived.

Rowena and Lupinski looked at each other and then looked at the door Scales had just disappeared through.

Lupinsli said, "I don't believe it. He's flipped, I mean entirely off his rocker. Is he on amphetamines or something?"

Rowena, still staring at the door said, "No, of course not……., well, at least I don't think so."

"I'm telling you something's different. You don't look like that unless you are sick or doing something to your body other than eating. And since when did he find religion. That praise the Lord thing, where did that come from?"

Phil Overholt walked away from the departing crowd and stood next to Rowena and Lupinski. "Some hooters, huh."

They both looked at him without comment.

Overholt pulled a cigarette from his shirt pocket and fiddled with it without lighting. "He serious about this online stuff? How we supposed to recruit when all the kid's got to do is sit

181

in his bedroom playing computer games?..... You issue this month's commission checks yet? I might as well start looking for another place to hang my hat. What about you, Lupinski, you movin' on?"

Rowena and Lupinski were still contemplating which question to answer first when Lisa Calmwater walked up and looped her arm through Phil's.

Phil smiled, "Nice show; great moves; maybe you could....."

Lisa interrupted, "You haven't paid your tab in over two months. Don't make me send Buster around to collect."

"Come on, Lisa, cut me a little slack. Things have been a little tight lately. How about I come in tonight and ...."

Lisa interrupted again as she turned to walk away, "Don't come in unless you bring cash, and I don't mean just for tonight, I mean pay up." As an afterthought, she turned to Rowena, "You think Jim is acting a little strange? He looks a little, I don't know, wore out. And then, what's with the praise the Lord mumbo jumbo, he gone goofy on us or something? Oh well," she gave one more glance at Overholt and said sternly, "don't forget what I said," and walked away.

Overholt gave a sheepish grin and walked away in the opposite direction.

Rowena said, "What a pair, no wonder this place is falling apart."

Lupinski took Rowena's arm, "Come on, we're going to talk to the good doctor and find out what's going on."

"Oh no," Rowena resisted, "I'm just a babysitter in this whole mess, I don't need to get involved any more than I already am."

"Just back me up, you don't have to say anything, I'll ask all the questions."

Rowena sighed and followed Lupinski through the door and up the stairs. They stood in front of Scales office door with a gold plate declaring *Dr. James Scales, President and CEO.* The closed door revealed only muted conversation. Lupinski reached for the door handle.

"Don't you dare," Rowena whispered, "you knock first."

Lupinski ignored her demand and twisted the knob and the door opened a few inches. They could only see half of the room but could hear Scales pleading with someone in almost crying tones.

"Please Cinderella, I need you; it's been almost a week. I can't take it, please."

Lupinski looked at Rowena and lipped *Cinderella?* Then he pushed the door a little more. The desk came into view and they could see Scales leaning over in his chair, his bare back exposed but his head not visible.

Rowena's first thought was, *God I hope he has pants on.*

"But Cinderella," Scales voice seemed to be breaking with emotion, "I can't wait that long, I need to come to Momma."

Rowena put her hand over her mouth like she was going to puke and turned to run but Lupinski grabbed her arm and said, "Oh no."

Suddenly, Scales head popped up, his sunken eyes bright with rage and his bare chest, shaved and red, heaving up and down, he screamed, "What the fuck are you doing here. *Get out, now."* Then he crouched back down and said, "Not you, not you, it's some asshole in my office; not you babe....... Babe....? Cin....? Scales came up standing tall and threw the phone at Lupinski.

183

Rowena thought, *Thank God he has underwear on, although..... Oh my God.*

Scales started to climb over the desk coming after Lupinski and then saw Rowena standing behind him. Standing on his desk, towering over them he yelled, "Get out, both of you, get out. This is a private office; private, do you understand, private. That means me, not you." Scales looked down and saw the protrusion in his underwear and tried to hide it with his hand, then jumped back into his chair behind the desk and sat down.

Rowena said, "I got to go."

Lupinski again grabbed her arm. "Oh no, we've come this far, we're going to finish it."

Scales yelled again, "Get out, and give me my phone back."

Lupinski picked up the phone that had bounced off the wall and slowly moved toward the desk and laid it on the edge. "Dr. Scales, we just want to talk to you for a minute. We know you are busy, but......"

Scales yelled in a soprano quiver, *"Geeeet out."*

Rowena peaked around Lupinski. "Jim, I know you are under a lot of stress, but, come on, put some clothes on. We just want to know you are okay."

"Don't I look okay? Didn't I look okay out there? This is my *private* office. If I want to run around in my underwear, I will. Now, get out."

Rowena continued, "But Jim, have you looked in the mirror lately? I'm worried about you. We've been friends for a long time. You can tell me. You want Randy to leave so we can talk?"

Scales face was getting redder by the second. This time he picked up a marble pen holder he had been given as a parting gift by the management of Super Value when the store closed and heaved it at the same wall the phone had hit and smashed it to pieces.

This time Rowena grabbed Lupinski's arm. "Okay, that's enough, let's go."

As they closed the door they could hear Scales talking to himself. "Crazy fuckers think they can just walk in here, well they can't."

*

Rowena and Randal Lupinski sat in Ralphie's Bar and Grill on Main Street trying to reconcile what they had just witnessed.

Lupinski said, "Was he talking to his wife?"

Rowena looked at Lupinski shaking her head, "And you've had how many years of college? You're kidding right. You think he calls his wife Cinderella, or his momma? Jeez, Randy, wake up. It's probably one of the hookers he sees. My guess is he's in love with one of them."

"Does he still have to pay?" Lupinski asked seriously, taking a drink of his Coke.

Rowena slapped her forehead in exasperation, "How would I know if he has to pay. Wow, sometimes I wonder about you. I guess you'll have to ask Dr. Scales. Just make sure he's not carrying."

"Carrying what?"

"Sometimes you amaze me, you know that. Are you really this naïve or is it an act? Carrying a gun, packing iron, concealed weapon; now you understand?"

185

This got Lupinski's attention. "You think he…., carries?"

"How should I know? If you were spending your time around hookers and pimps, wouldn't you?" She looked at Lupinski. "Forget I said that."

Lupinski took offense. "You think I'm some kind of prude, don't you? Well, I've been around guns. We, my dad and I, used to go to his club and shoot trap."

"Well, the next time I hear that trap shoots back, that experience might help, but for now, I'd stay out of the line of fire."

Rowena could see Lupinski was a little miffed by the way he strangled his Coke glass. "Look, I don't see that Jim's problems are anything we should be sticking our nose in. He'll come to his senses, *I hope.*"

"I've been thinking," Lupinski responded, "while you've been rattling my cage, maybe we should do an intervention."

"*A what,*" Rowena asked. "An invention, what's that? I mean, I know what an invention is, but what's that have to do with anything?"

"Inter…., an *inter*vention. It means we figure out a way to get Jim, Dr. Scales, out of his comfort zone and into a situation where he can get some help."

"Help with what?" Rowena asked cautiously.

"With whatever is wrong."

Rowena took a hard swig of her beer. "Look, you may think you are some kind of psychoanalyst because you've had a bunch of college, but let me explain reality; men go through fazes like this. Like I said, he's probably infatuated with some hooker. He'll find out it's wrong, and then, well, he'll be back to normal, I hope."

186

Lupinski responded, "I can tell by the way you said that, you don't believe it. Look, you said you have been his friend for twenty some years, don't you think you owe it to him to try to help?"

"Help with what?" Rowena asked again.

"With his problem, he's not the first guy to go off the deep end when it comes to women. I still think we consider an intervention of some sort. Find out where he is meeting this, what did he call her, Cindy something?"

Rowena answered almost under her breath, "Cinderella."

"Yeah, Cinderella; we confront him when he's getting ready to meet her; you, me, maybe some other close friends; try to convince him to give it up, come home and get some counseling or something."

Rowena stared straight ahead. "And what if he just says, hey you're all fired and leave me alone; what do you do then?"

Lupinski didn't answer for a minute and then said, "I'm not sure, but at least we tried."

Rowena dug deeper, "And what about Janet, his wife? While you are intervening, or whatever, what do you tell his wife? Hey Janet, we caught your husband with a thousand dollar hooker and we intervened. I'm sure she will appreciate that, while she's on her way down to her lawyer's office....... I don't know why I'm even having this conversation, it's nuts. I'm going home; at least my husband is sane, most of the time."

"Okay, maybe it is a little over the top, but let's give it some thought. At least let me know the next time you think he's meeting Cind......, you know who I mean."

CHAPTER 29

Marla Todd and Mary Good sat in Marla's car at the Hinkley MacDonald's sharing an order of French fries. Marla said, "I'm going to do it. I've got most of it figured out."

Mary responded quickly, "Don't even say that. You are not going to do anything. We've had this conversation too many times. It's illegal, it's immoral, it's just wrong."

"I don't care. It's only wrong if it doesn't work. And for that matter, I don't think it's illegal. Why is it illegal if someone wants to give you something?"

Mary sighed, "When you coerce or threaten someone, that's not giving on their part, it's called ransom or extortion. We've been through this too many times, Mar."

"But see, I'm not going to demand anything, like, I'm just going to suggest it. Like, I'm just going to say," Marla tilted her head and put her palm on her cheek, "Dr. Scales, honey, it sure would be nice if you gave Mary Good a scholarship……"

Mary interrupted, laughing at Marla's portrayal, "Or I'll show your wife these pictures, that how it goes?"

"Something like that, but not necessarily."

"I know we have had some laughs over this, but I'm serious," Mary put on a stern expression, "you are not going to do this. If you want to continue to be my friend, you have to promise you will not do this."

"Eat your fries, Hats," Marla said and smiled.

*

"Buster, this is the slutster," Marla said into her phone lying on her bed. "No, I don't need any weed. Like, I need a favor...... Yeah, well remember when I did that thing for you? .... I can't help it if he didn't like you. Who do you think I am, like the gay cupid? .... Yeah, well back at you....... It would be a lot easier if you liked women. Just shut up and listen, okay? Actually, I need, like, two things. You know how you take pictures of the girls at the club, and, like, sell 'um. I need you to take some pictures for me........ Don't worry, I'll do you right..... Yeah, I'll call him again. And anyway, after I get done with the pictures, they'll be like gold for you........ I don't want to talk about it on the phone........ No, it's not illegal, and anyway, since when do you care?"

*

"Mr. Lizardo, this is Janet Scales..... Scales, you followed my husband and caught him with the hooker....... Yeah, *that* Scales. I need you to do one more thing for me; I want you to set up a rendezvous with his hooker in this area. It doesn't have to be in Hinkley, but maybe in the Falls, Cougar Falls, about twenty miles away…….. Why can't you?...... I'm not going to shoot him, or her; you think I'm nuts?........ I know you don't want any part of it. You won't; I just want to see his face when I catch him. You can even tell his hooker what's going on……… Oh, she will when you offer her three grand plus expenses……… Okay, make it four, but only half up front. As soon as I walk in, she can get up and leave, no strings attached……… Just find her and make the offer. Tell her to tell him she's coming to see her sick mother or something, and just has to see him again. There's a Best Western near the interstate on the north end of town. They have a bar and restaurant. That's a perfect place. It's close enough that by the next day everyone in Hinkley will know about it."

*

"Dr. Hunter, this is Randall Lupinski, your graduate intern, remember…..? Yeah, do you have a moment?....... Thank you for noticing, I tried to be involved in all of my graduate studies, but found your lectures to be most stimulating……. Oh, the reason I called, yes, I'll get right to the point; I doubt you are aware, but I am the dean of the business school at a small community college………. Well, thank you, I feel it is a remarkable achievement as well……….. It's Hinkley Community College……… Understandable, you've not heard of it, it's a small school, but growing rapidly. But, the reason I called; I have a disturbing situation with the President of our college……… I understand that you can't get involved in faculty disagreements.

I'm not asking you to get involved; I just need your advice or opinion with regard to the psychological or mental condition I am dealing with.......... No, not mine, the President; you see, he has, how shall I say, become obsessed with, uh, having sexual encounters with prostitutes......... How do I know? I've been told by associates that are close to him......... No, I don't think he's just horny, he has a wife........ No, I haven't talked to her....... I really don't think I'm in the position........ Okay, If the opportunity presents itself, I will address the issue with her, but........ No, she's not that attractive, but....... Okay, I'll give you that point, he may be trying to......... I understand it's common for a man to seek, support, as you put it, but in this case, well, it's way beyond that. Bluntly, he's spending a couple grand a week on call girls in Chicago......... Yes, I said a couple grand........ No, I don't know how much he gets paid as President....... Well, I suppose, if something happens to him, we will need a replacement........ Yes, I'll be sure to mention your name, but, right now, I would like to know if there is a common diagnosis for, you know,......... Okay, you want to call it chasing tail, that's what we'll call it. But I'm looking for a more medical sounding term; something I can actually apply if it is necessary to create a legal document........ We haven't gotten that far yet, but yes, I promise I will mention your name. But, psychologically speaking is there a term for his condition? .... That's good, hold on a minute, I need to write this down; *libido fulfillment through sexual pleasure*, go on, *that is expressed in conscious activity, commonly referred to as sexual drive.* Is that it? .... Yes, I think that is what I am looking for. See, we are thinking about doing an intervention, and hopefully

191

referring him to counseling. I think once we confront him and he realizes he has a problem, he will take some action on his own......... Well, I suppose he would have to take a leave of absence......... I know, I'll be sure to mention it."

CHAPTER 30

The first week of classes was fast approaching and Jim Scales had not been seen since the faculty pep talk meeting. Rowena was beginning to wonder if his personal issues had pushed him over the edge and his wife had had him committed. But, on the other hand, in a town this size, those types of activities did not go unnoticed and she would have heard the news ten times over by now.

Billy Bob Redbone passed through her door and plopped down in the folding chair in front of her desk. "What's this I hear about some kind of hearing in front of the accreditation board?"

"All I know is we received a notice, but it's not for a week, so you've got time to get your act together."

Billy Bob raised his eyebrows and tried to look offended. "What act? I'll tell you this, if Scales doesn't make me a doctor this semester and step up to the plate with some money, I'm movin' on."

"And what, you going back to the butcher shop? Oh wait, the butcher shop closed, so that leaves Wal-Mart. Billy Bob, you've never had it so good, so before you start jumping ship, I'd check to see if there are any oars in the lifeboat." Rowena went back to her crossword puzzle ignoring Redbone.

"There's other schools that need professorin', you can bet on that. Where is he anyway, haven't seen him all week. Not that anybody misses him standing around checkin' his watch like we're on a time clock or somethin'. By the way, what's the name of that nurse that comes by the day care once a week? She is one fine specimen."

Rowena slapped her pencil down. "Redbone, get out of here, I've got more important things to do that to listen to your crass comments."

Over Redbone's shoulder she saw Jim Scales practically run by her office and then heard his office door slam shut.

Redbone turned, but too late. "Who was that?"

"Dun know," Rowena responded staring at her crossword.

"Sounded like Scales office door," Redbone said standing. "Think I'll go talk at him a bit."

"Uh, I wouldn't recommend that right now. You might want to give him a little time to settle in."

"My grand pappy always told me, you think it's time, it must be the right time, because if you wait, it'll be too late." Redbone turned and walked out heading toward Scales office.

The next thing Rowena heard was Scales yelling, "Get out, get out of here you idiot and leave me alone."

Redbone came walking back down the hall and as he passed he said, "Somethin' ain't right with him, that's for shore. He sick or somethin'?"

Rowena settled back into her chair and concentrated on her cross word puzzle. Her phone rang, the main line to the school. "Hinkley Community College, how may I direct your call?"

"This is Sharon from the Cougar Falls Best Western, a Dr. Scales made a reservation for Thursday requesting our suite and we thought it was reserved, but now it has opened up and we have reserved it for him. I have been calling the number he gave but it has been busy forever. He used a credit card from the college, so I thought I might be able to reach him through you."

"I will be happy to give him the message, thank you." Rowena scribbled a note and set it aside, not really ready to confront Dr. Jim in his current state of mind."

Randy Lupinski stepped into her office. "Hi, Rowena, I thought I saw Dr. Scales come in the back door, he in?"

"I think so, but I wouldn't recommend bothering him right now, he's a little testy. I'm holding his calls and his messages for the time being."

Lupinski looked over her desk at her note pad. "What's that, something about a reservation at the Best Western? Is that in Chicago?"

Rowena turned the pad over. "None of your business. Anyway, it's not Chicago, it's the one in the Falls."

"Really, he's meeting her there, in Cougar Falls?"

"I don't know who he's meeting or why. Just drop it, it's none of your business."

"Yeah, but Rowena," Lupinski said, "this is perfect for what we talked about. It's close enough we can get somebody from his church; maybe one of his close friends from the club; it's perfect."

"Are you crazy, you still on this invention thing?" Rowena looked at the door realizing it was still open. "Close that door." She waited for him to sit down and lowered her voice. "No way am I going to do that. You saw how he was the last time we tried to talk to him. What do you think will happen when we surprise him like that? You are liable to get shot, if not by him, by his hooker."

Lupinski continued as though Rowena hadn't offered any objection. "I've been doing some research and found this is not uncommon, especially in men his age. It's a libido issue, but most men don't let it get so out of hand. I think you are right, I think he's become infatuated with one of the, the girls he sees, and it's taken hold of his senses. He just needs someone to get in front of him and bring him back, get him thinking straight again. That's what the intervention can do, get him talking to the right counselor about his problem. It's just like alcohol or drugs; one has to admit to the problem before one can overcome it."

Rowena interrupted, "Well, this is *one* that's not going to get involved."

"What night is the reservation?"

"It's Thur....... I told you it's none of your business," Rowena said sternly, "now get out."

Lupinski once again ignored her request. "That doesn't leave much time. You nail down the time and I'll work on the other details. He's Catholic, maybe I can get Father Cardone to go along, that'd be a good touch, don't you think?"

Rowena slapped her hand on the desk in exasperation, "Don't you listen, I'm not doing this. Just forget about it."

"Okay, we're all set. Call me when you find out the time, then we'll coordinate the transportation." Lupinski got up and started for the door, "Oh yeah, maybe you should talk to his wife too," and exited closing the door.

*

"Okay, Buster, I got your message, like, what did you find out?" Marla asked, sitting in her car in the community college parking lot smoking a joint.

"I checked with all the girls here and at the other club, at least the ones that would talk to me there, and none of 'em even know him. And believe me, if he's spreading money around like you said, they would know about it. I called all the motels where I know the desk people, we slip them stuff so they will send their lonely customers to the club, and none of them say they have supplied him with any girls. The only hit I got was Carly, at the Best Western out on I-70, she said he made a reservation for Thursday; must be some kind of party because he reserved their only suite...." Buster yelled away from the phone, "What, okay, I'll be right there.... I gotta go slutster, some asshole's trying to feel up Malinda the cat lady."

Marla thought for a minute. "That sounds more like some kind of, like, school thing. Okay, I'll let you know when it's time for the picture thing."

Marla leaned back and took another hit. *It could work,* she thought, *if somehow we got him down in the bar, get close and snap a few pictures, it might work.*

CHAPTER 31

J erry Ringwald answered the door bell holding a can of Leinenkugel ale, wearing a Leinenkugel advertisement tee shirt, gym shorts and socks. "Father Cardone, what, you making house calls now? Pardon my casual dress, but hey, it's my house." Both men smiled at the candor. "Might as well come in, want a Leinie's?"

"That would be nice," Cardone answered and walked through the living room into the den and took a seat in Jerry's reserved recliner in front of the TV that was tuned to the baseball game and said to Jerry's back as he walked away for the beer, "The Sox winning? Tough year."

Rowena came out of the kitchen. "Who's at the....... Cardy, what are you doing here?"

"Nice to see you too," he responded, "just a courtesy call, and of course, a personal invitation to mass. I find the personal touch instills a much greater dose of guilt, don't you agree?"

Jerry came in with the Leinie's from the garage refrigerator and showing some frustration that his chair was unceremoniously taken, handed the beer to Cardone and sat down on the couch next to Rowena. Both stared at Cardone as he took a long draw of the beer.

Cardone looked at the pair and asked, "Well, how are we tonight?"

Neither answered.

"Like I said," Cardone continued realizing he would have to carry the conversation, "this is just a friendly visit; a chance to catch up and maybe talk about the issues at the school."

"Oh," Rowena said, like a big light bulb ignited in her head.

Jerry said, "What about the school?"

Rowena suddenly realizing where the conversation was headed tried to curve it in another direction. "Cardy visited the school the other day and, well, was quite impressed, *weren't you?*" Her emphasis and squinting eyes trying to send a message to Cardone.

It didn't work. "Rowena came to confession, something you might want to consider, Jerry, and we had a nice talk after about the school."

"*You went to confession?*" Jerry's shocked expression overwhelmed by his laughter. "I don't believe it."

"What's so hard to believe about that? Somebody around here has to show some remorse now and then for all your sins."

Jerry feigned shock, "You've got a lot'a room to talk."

"Now kids, fight nice," Cardone said smiling. "Anyway, after Row and I talked, I gave it some prayer time and asked a few questions around town. Do you know that there are almost five hundred students at that school?"

Rowena said under her breath, "Oh boy."

199

"And the average tuition is close to eight thousand dollars. I was shocked when I started doing the math. It didn't take too long to figure out how Jim Scales could afford that mansion he built." Cardone took another long draw on his beer. "Then I started hearing these rumors about Dr. Scales cavorting with, how shall I put it, ladies of the night all over the country and ...."

Rowena repeated, "Oh boy."

"Then I get a visit from this young Lupinski, handsome young man, mind you, expressing his concerns about...."

Rowena abruptly interrupted, "Maybe we shouldn't discuss this, I mean, rumors, that's all they are. How's the parish softball team doing? I understand they are in the playoffs."

Jerry said, "Whoa, wait a minute, I want to hear this. Scales is doing hookers, that what you said?"

"*Jerry,*" Rowena threatened, "not in front of Father."

"Father my butt, he brought it up."

Cardone continued, "Apparently, this problem, that is, Mr. Scales problem, has become serious enough that Mr. Lupinski, he's a trained psychologist by the way, feels someone needs to intervene and seek help for Jim."

"Who told you he's a trained psychologist?" Rowena asked. "He may have taken a couple psych classes in his time, but he's far from trained, I can tell you that."

Jerry leaned forward, "What do you mean he wants to intervene; he want to catch him in the act, doing it with a hooker?"

"*Jerry,* that's enough." Rowena stood up hoping to alert Cardone it was time to leave. I didn't work, so she sat back down.

200

"I don't think he has that in mind, but he does want to confront him and he hopes it will inspire some self evaluation." Cardone drained the beer and fumbled with the can, letting Jerry know it was empty.

"Want another?" Jerry asked.

"Sure, one more shouldn't hurt."

Rowena sighed and shook her head as Jerry left the room and whispered, "You have to bring all this up in front of him?"

"He's your husband, your soul mate; you don't think he should know what you are up to?"

"*I'm not up to anything*," Rowena continued to whisper almost spitting out the words. "I told Randy I didn't want anything to do with this, and I still don't."

"I think it's too late for that. He says Thursday you and he, and now me, are going to meet Mr. Scales and have a frank discussion about his problem." Jerry walked back in and handed Cardone the cold beer. Cardone continued, "We were just discussing how Rowena and I and this Randall are going to meet with Mr. Scales and hopefully have a frank discussion about his issues."

Jerry looked at Rowena and grinned, "Me too."

Rowena slumped back in the couch and said, "Oh boy."

CHAPTER 32

Marla pulled down the lane to the Good residence. The serene scene was unchanged as she parked some distance from the house. Mr. Good stepped onto the porch and stared without any visible recognition of Marla's presence. Marla gave a petite wave from her car window and waited. Mr. Good finally returned into the house and Mary replaced his position on the porch, apparently waiting for Marla to approach. Marla waved again and motioned for Mary to come to the car.

"Hi Mar, why don't you come in?" Mary said approaching the car and then grew stone cold when she got close enough to see Marla's attire. "Oh no, you're not......, are you?"

Marla wore a low cut halter with silk camisole, leather short skirt and black lace hosiery. She had colored her hair jet black and wore hoop earrings. "It's now or never. I'm on my way. I just wanted someone other than Buster to know where I'm going."

"*You are not doing this.* I will not allow you to do this. It is not right, Marla, and you know that."

Marla started the car. "I'm sorry, but it's all set. I'll call you tonight and tell you what happens."

"Marla, if you do this, do not call me ever again. I do not want to be your friend. I do not want to be any part of this." A tear meandered down Mary's cheek.

"Aw, come on Hats, it's no big deal, like, it's just a gag. I'll surprise him, have a laugh or two, and that's it. Buster gets a couple long shots and bingo, it's done."

Mary started to plead, "He will recognize you in an instant. What do you do then? He's seen you every day for a year. He's even seen you at his house working. You think black hair makes a difference?"

"It's not going to matter. Once I sit down next to him, he's, like, had, assuming Buster gets the shots."

"He will see you coming. You think he isn't going to recognize that tattoo on your chest?"

Marla tried to pull the camisole up to cover the tattoo. "I know, that's one I wish I had a do over. Don't know what I was thinking. Anyway, I'll think of some way to get his attention diverted. Like, I'll sit down with my back to him first; something like that."

Mary marched around to the passenger door and got in. "I'm going."

"No way," Marla protested.

Mary crossed her arms and stared straight ahead in silence.

"Hats, listen, like, if I get in trouble, it don't matter."

"Doesn't," Mary corrected, "doesn't matter."

"Yeah, whatever. If I get in trouble, it's just another stupid stunt, like, it's normal. But if you are part of it, well, it could hurt you. Then you might never get to go to a real school......, so get out."

"I will not." Mary continued to stare straight ahead.

Marla stared straight ahead with her hands on the steering wheel and pondered her predicament. "If you go, you have to sit in the car."

Silence.

"You have to promise."

Silence.

"Did you feed the ducks?"

Silence.

"Hats, sometimes you can be a real pain," Marla put the car in gear and made a sweeping turn. "You are staying in the car and that's final."

CHAPTER 33

Richie Lizardo sat in the Best Western parking lot eating a warm tuna salad sandwich he had purchased at the seven eleven an hour before. So far the only person entering the *Twilight Moods* lounge entrance was a large skin head with tattoos covering every visible part of his body, including his bald head, carrying a briefcase. The purported meeting time was four o'clock, some fifteen minutes away and he was starting to get the typical stake out feeling that it had all been a waste of time. Valerie Smanski, a. k. a. Cinderella, had yet to show her face, which was not a surprise as well. He only had one task and that was to give Valerie the other half of the two grand he promised once she played her final role in this nasty web of deceit.

Bingo, Lizardo thought as a Cadillac Escalade pulled into the parking lot. The tinted windows obscured the identity of the driver, but he recognized the plate as belonging to Jim Scales.

After a prolonged delay, Scales, dressed casually in an open collar golf shirt and slacks, stepped out, gave a cursory look around the parking lot as if he suspected this could be some sort of trap, and made a fast pace to the lounge entrance.

Lizardo took another bite and leaned back, satisfied at least that part of the plan was working.

Another vehicle, a minivan, pulled into the lot and parked well away from the lounge entrance. The occupants were visible but they didn't immediately exit, appearing to be discussing their next move, occasionally pointing to the lounge door. Soon a fat clergyman, maybe a priest, stepped out of the van followed by three other adults. They mingled at the front of the van, each periodically checking their respective watches. Having deliberated for some time, they all climbed back into the van and made no attempt to leave.

A third vehicle, belching blue smoke, rambled into the parking lot and stopped in an awkward angle taking up three spaces well away from the entrance. It was far enough away from Lizardo that he couldn't make out the two occupants intentions, but there seemed to be a lot of movement in the car and he imagined it to be some kids hoping to be unobserved in their delinquent activity.

The main players in his act, Janet Scales and Valerie, still needed to arrive or the whole plan was a bust. Fortunately, money in advance was money in the bank.

*

"That's his SUV, the Escalade; Janet drives the one that's more like a car. He must be in there," Rowena said staring at the entrance to the lounge.

Father Cardone said, "Let's go, it's getting hot in here."

"Hold your horses, Cardy," Rowena said, squirming a bit, "we can't just walk in there, all four of us, it'll look like a parade."

"Yeah," Jerry said, "and Father, you get to be the elephant."

"Hush, Jerry," Rowena scolded. "What do you think *Randall,* this was your idea?"

"Well, uh, I don't know; you're right, we can't just all waltz in there……., maybe one of us goes and checks it out. If he's sitting there with the hook……., his date, then there's a signal and we all come in."

Rowena sighed like a deflating balloon. "Well let's see," she looked at Cardone, "a Priest walks into a hooker bar, *that* shouldn't draw any attention." She looked back at Lupinski. "You walk in; God knows he wouldn't recognize you, his employee, Dean of Admissions. I walk in, same effect, only worse since I'm not a hooker. That leaves Jerry," she turned and looked at her husband, "trouble is, he may never come out once they put a beer in front of him."

Jerry opened the car door, anxious to get out in the air and get a beer. "I'll be out in a flash. Let's see, if I walk out and just stand there with my hands in my pockets; or no, if I point at the sign……, that means not to come in. If I walk out, let's see, and bend over like I'm gonna puke, that means you should come in."

"*Jerry,* just walk out and wave, okay. Jeez, you're not 007. And don't sit in there and drink a beer while we roast out here. Go in and come back out." Rowena watched him head for the entrance. "This is a mistake, I can feel it."

207

As the door to the bar closed behind Jerry Ringwald, the door on the rusty car across the parking lot opened and a girl in a short skirt, heels and lace stockings stepped out and headed for the entrance.

"That must be her," Lupinski said, straining to get a better look.

"Quit gawking," Rowena said straining as well.

Cardone said, "We might as well follow her in. At least we know what she's here for."

"We should wait until Jerry gives us the signal," Rowena said skeptically. "Maybe she's a different...., one."

"If she is a different one, you want Jerry in there by himself?" Lupinski asked.

"Good point," Rowena said hurriedly getting out of the car.

*

Lizardo had half fallen asleep, but occasionally opened one eye to see if there was any change in the parking lot. He just caught the girl in the high heels opening the door to the lounge and straightened up trying to get a good look. As the door closed he searched the parking lot for Valerie's car without success. *How did she get here?* He looked back at the door as the Priest and two others pushed through, again wondering if he was imagining the vision of Valerie, or maybe it was someone else.

A black Cadillac sedan roared into the parking lot, slid to a stop, and then sped up again heading straight for his car. Janet Scales slammed on the brakes, parking directly in front of him and rolled out of the car.

"Is he in there? Is she here?" Janet wailed as he opened his window. Janet's chest heaved up and down as she twisted her neck to look at the lounge entrance and then back at Lizardo.

"He's in there," Lizardo responded, "but I'm not sure about the girl."

"Why not? That's your job. Get out of the car and go find out. What are you waiting for, me to do it? That's what I pay you for, to know what's going on."

Lizardo said, "Okay, calm down. I'll check it out. I don't think she's here yet, but I'll find out and come back out and let you know. You don't have a gun or anything, do you?"

"If I did, I'd probably shoot you. Four thousand dollars and you don't even know what's going on."

"Alright, alright, get back in your car. I'll find out and be right back."

*

Lizardo cautiously entered the outside door stepping into a foyer that led to another lounge entrance door. He stopped, letting his eyes adjust to the dim light and then opened the door to the bar. The outer walls of the room had booths surrounding some cocktail tables with the bar at the far end. As his vision adjusted, he noted the mini-van group crowded into a booth at the farthest point from the bar. Another booth was occupied by the skinhead, apparently asleep with four empty beer bottles spread out in front of him. The girl, definitely not Valerie, sat at the end of the bar fidgeting with a napkin and a glass of water.

Scales sat staring at the wall behind the bar cradling a martini. Noting the inactivity and the absence of Valerie, he stepped back out into the foyer hallway.

Valerie stepped into the foyer meeting Lizardo head on.

"What's going on? Where's the pigeon?" Valerie asked indignantly. "Where's my money? I'm not going in there until I get my money."

"He's sitting at the bar," Lizardo said trying to exert some authority. "Just go in and sit down. His old lady's outside. As soon as she comes in, you can leave. I'll have your money outside; I'll be in my car."

"Yeah, right," Valerie said, "and while you're at it, pin the kick me in the ass sign on my back. I'm not doing anything until I get my money."

"Okay, okay, calm down. It's not like you're do'in this for peanuts. I'll go get the money and be right back. I don't know how long I can hold his old lady back. She's like a steam engine ready to blow, so let's get this over with."

Lizardo went out leaving Valerie to wait in the foyer. She leaned against the wall and lit a cigarette underneath the no smoking sign and relaxed.

A girl with long auburn hair, halter top, short leather skirt and lace stockings came out of the bar, almost bumping into Valerie. Their eyes locked and then the girl looked away, an embarrassed expression.

"Don't worry," Valerie said, "I'm not working the bar. I'm just here to see someone; I'll be gone in a few minutes. Any luck in there?"

The girl looked at her in a strange way but didn't answer.

"Like I said, don't worry, you'll never see me again; this place is all yours. Not sure how you can make it working a dog like this. You're nice looking, you ever think about moving up, I mean to the big league? I could set you up in one of the rooms I work in Chicago; guarantee five hundred a night; interested?"

The girl looked confused, almost like she was about to cry, turned and walked back into the bar.

*

Lizardo returned to the foyer, handed Valerie an envelope that she promptly opened and counted out ten one hundred dollar bills.

"Satisfied?" Lizardo asked incredulously.

"Yeah, let's get this over with. I've got to be back by ten; another appointment."

"High volume day at the old crotch hotel, huh?"

Valerie looked at Lizardo with a laser stare. "It keeps me out of the cesspool you swim in." She turned and walked into the bar.

Janet Scales burst through the outer door just as the inner door closed behind Valerie. "What's going on in here? You having some kind of party with my money? Is she in there?"

Lizardo held up his hands palms out. "Quiet down, she just went in there. Give her a minute to get settled." He looked down at Janet's large purse hanging heavily under her stretched arm. "What's in there?" He said sternly pointing at the purse.

"Nothing, let's go."

Lizardo, now more cautious than curious said, "We'll just wait another minute or two."

211

*

Valerie moved through the door with cautious steps. The room opened up before her. The skinhead snored in the corner booth. The Priest and accompanying party huddled in another booth. The girl she had spoken to in the hall now sat at the end of the bar and Jim Scales sat in the middle of the bar, leaning back with his hands clasped on his chest. She was about to move into position at the bar when the other girl rose and moved down and sat next to Scales.

She's making a move on my mark, Valerie thought, the hair on her neck starting to stand up and the burn of distaste growing in her throat. She started to take an aggressive step toward the bar but stopped when she saw the group in the booth in the corner all raise and head in the same direction.

At the same moment, the door to the lounge lurched open and Janet scales bounded into the room, pushed Valerie aside while looking one way then another, surveying the room until she saw Scales sitting at the bar with a girl at his side. She started toward the bar on a collision course with the other group making the same pace.

Valerie, a seasoned veteran of bar cat fights and family brawls instinctively realized it was time to exit and turned for the door, only to meet Lizardo following Janet Scales.

"I'm out of here," Valerie said stepping around Lizardo. "This is gonna get ugly in a hurry."

Lizardo quickly looked the situation over and said, "You're right," and followed her out of the door.

*

212

Jim Scales, realizing he was not alone at the bar and also realizing it wasn't Cinderella sitting next to him, turned to the girl and said, "Who are you?" Before he received an answer he was surrounded. He turned with his elbow on the back of his chair and observed Father Cardone, whom he barely knew but recognized from a few wedding ceremonies he had attended; next to him Jerry somebody, couldn't put the name to the face; straining to look behind him he found Rowena and Lupinski, both with gaunt expressions staring at him. "What is this, some kind of party I didn't get invited to?" Then he looked again at the girl next to him and again asked, "And who are you?"

Rowena started to announce their intentions, since everyone else seemed to be mute on the subject, when she took a closer look at the girl and brought her hand to her mouth, "Oh my god in heaven, it's, it's," she leaned closer for a better look, "it's Mary Good. I don't believe it."

"Who?" Scales asked again, separating himself from the girl with a little push.

Janet Scales, with a move an NFL linebacker would be proud of, pushed Cardone in one direction and Jerry Ringwald in the other, creating separation for her wide presentation. She pulled a giant rubber penis from her purse and proceeded to clobber Jim Scales over the head yelling, "Remember this, you whore mongering twit; what you gave me for our first wedding anniversary; is it funny now?"

Buster, aroused by all the commotion, stumbled toward the action, jumped up on the bar and took over head shots of the pummeling.

213

Marla, wondering why Buster wouldn't answer his phone, stepped through the door to the bar dressed in Mary's flowered dress, and took in the scene. Of most interest and importance she noted, was the bartender on the phone with whom she perceived to be the police. She scurried through the room and approached next to Mary. "Hats….., Hat's, let's go……, now." She grabbed Mary's arm and wrenched her away from the flailing penis. At the same time she pulled on Buster's pant leg as he continued to shoot photos standing on the bar, "Buster, let's go, I think the law's on the way."

*

Father Cardone, in shock at first and then intrigued by the brutality of the giant penis, finally grabbed Janet's arm and stopped her two fisted onslaught. "Janet, that's enough, I think you made your point."

Janet, her chest heaving up and down and sweat dripping from her brow asked like nothing had happened, "Father Cardone, nice to see you." Then she looked around at the rest of the group and asked, "What's going on here?"

Scales, hunched down with his arms over his head to repel the pummeling said, "Yeah, what's going on here?"

Lupinski finally decided it was time to insert his intellectual interpretation of the situation. "You see, Dr. Scales, we are here to intervene in your, well, your problem; libido problem, that is."

"His *what?*" Janet Scales screamed. "Is that her name, libido?" Janet wheeled around looking at the empty room

214

grasping the giant penis with both hands for more action. "Where'd libido go?" She raised the giant penis up in the air. "I'll show her what his problem is."

"No, no, no, Mrs. Scales, you don't understand. Dr. Scales is suffering from, well, it's kind of like a disease, of the mind. He feels he needs to feed his libido, his sexual desire by, well, using women."

Jim Scales said, "*What?* Where did you get that crap?" He turned to Janet, "Look Janet, I'm sorry, but I don't love you anymore, I love Cinderella."

"*Cinder who?* What about libido, you love her too. How many other whores do you love?" Janet started laughing like a crazed hyena, threw the giant penis down and turned and walked toward the door. She turned and said, "You know what you are really going to love? You are really going to love how this all plays out in divorce court. Yeah, and be sure to invite Cinder and Libido, they should get a big kick out of it too."

The door closed and the group, with exception of Scales who was still cowering in his seat, stood and watched her leave. Within a few seconds the door opened again and two police officers walked in, both with night sticks drawn, ready for a bar fight.

Rowena said, "Oh boy."

Father Cardone crossed himself and said a silent prayer.

Lupinski stepped behind Rowena and whispered, "What do we do now?"

Jerry Ringwald whistled at the bar tender and asked for another beer.

Jim Scales stood up and said, "Officers, arrest these people."

The two officers approached cautiously, surveying the scene. Officer Crowly, the younger looking of the two, noticed the giant penis on the floor and poked at it with his night stick. He looked at Officer Smith and said, "Wow, that's some prick."

Jim Scales stood, brushed at his shirt and pants as if ridding himself of the problem and continued, "I want these people arrested."

"For what?" Officer Smith asked.

"For, I don't know, assault; inciting a riot; trespassing, I don't care."

"How did they assault you?" Crowly asked, balancing on his toes with his night stick pinned behind his back.

"I was attacked with that giant penis." Scales pointed at the rubber object on the floor.

Crowly had to feign coughing to hide his laughter and Smith, the obviously more mature officer carried on the inquiry. "So Mr......."

"Dr., Dr. Scales."

"Okay, Dr. Scales, which one of these......, perpetrators, assaulted you with the, the giant penis? Was this a sexual assault, that is, with the giant penis?"

Father Cardone couldn't keep quiet any longer. "My good man, I find that insinuation extremely troubling."

Officer Smith held up his hand in front of Cardone, "You'll have your turn. I think this is going to take a while. We don't get many giant penis assaults, as a matter of fact, this may be a first."

Crowly had to turn away and rub the laughter tears from his eyes.

216

"No it wasn't a sexual assault, my wife beat me over the head with it while these people watched. They are, what do you call it, accessories to the crime." Scales once again brushed the wrinkles from his shirt and straightened the crease in his pants and said, "I have to go, so do your job and arrest these people."

"Just sit back down Dr. Scales. You've made a serious accusation here, that being assault with a giant penis. So we are going to have to investigate and find out some of the facts; like, how did the giant penis get here in the first place; was the giant penis brought here as a premeditated act, or was it brought here for another purpose and in a fit of giant penis furry, used as a weapon instead of, well, whatever you use a giant penis for?"

Crowly couldn't hold on any longer and burst out laughing before moving down the bar to stand near the bartender who was in awe of the whole proceeding. Crowly crossed his arms and said, "Just sit back and enjoy this. He could work this routine until shift change."

Scales looked down the bar at Crowly and then at Smith. "So you guys think this is funny, a real riot; something to talk about back at the precinct I suppose?"

Smith ignored Scales criticism and turned to Rowena. "So, you must be Mrs. Dr. Scales. Let's hear your side of the giant penis attack."

"*What*, are you kidding? I'm not his wife, and I didn't have anything to do with him getting clobbered with that thing."

"Well, if you didn't do it, who did?" Smith looked around the room and said, "This isn't one of those man wife things, is it? One of you guys his wife?"

"Perhaps I can explain," Father Cardone interrupted.

217

Smith sized up the Priest and said, "Okay reverend, let's hear it."

"First, I'm a Priest at the Parrish in Hinkley. Dr. Scales wife left just before you came in so I'm afraid your so called perpetrator is no longer present. Our, that is Rowena, Jerry, Randall and my interest in this situation was an effort to intervene in Dr. Scales personal issues involving use of prostitutes to satisfy his....., what did you call it Randall? Randall is a trained psychologist."

Scales yelled, *"My what? He's a what?"*

Lupinski said, "His need to satisfy his libido inadequacy."

"He isn't a trained psychologist," Scales blubbered, almost in shock, "he sells student tuition at my school. And what's this libido crap? You guys followed me here to do what? Look officer......, what's your name?"

"Smith, Officer Smith."

"Look Officer Smith, I came in here to have a cocktail before going home. From what I can tell, this group of nitwits conspired with my wife to come here and assault me. If that isn't grounds for an arrest, I don't know what is. So do your job, I'm leaving." Scales started to get up again and Smith put his big hand on his shoulder and pushed him back down.

"Did any of you hit Dr. Scales with the giant penis?" Smith asked.

Everyone shook their head signaling a defiant no while Jerry Ringwald ordered another beer and asked Rowena, "You want one?"

"God yes. What about you Cardy?"

Cardone sighed and sat down at the bar. "I'll have a Leinie's and a Jack chaser."

218

Officer Smith stepped over to the giant penis on the floor. "Better keep this for evidence."

Crowly looked at the bartender and said, "Well, I'd say that about wraps up the investigation. Looks like you've got some thirsty customers."

*

Marla and Mary sat in the rusty car watching the door to the lounge. It opened and they both slumped down, peeking over the dashboard. The officers came out and got into the cruiser and after some discussion and apparent laughter, drove away.

Mary slumped in the passenger seat. "Mrs. Ringwald recognized me right away. Why would she be here, and Mr. Lupinski? And I was afraid Dr. Scales would recognize *you*, and look what happened. What do we do now? We'll both get expelled."

"I knew I should never have let you talk me into changing places." Marla stared at nothing trying to make sense of the turn of events. "It still could work, Buster got some great shots. Did you see her whacking him with that rubber penis?"

"Is that what it was?"

"Yeah," Marla replied starting to laugh, "never seen anything like that before."

"Look," Mary said pointing at the entrance, "get down."

Scales stomped out of the door and double timed to his Escalade, burning rubber leaving the parking lot.

Marla said, "He doesn't look too happy, Hats."

219

Mary thought for a minute and then said, "Did you see the other lady that was standing outside the inner door?"

"I saw a tall girl, lotta makeup, and a guy leave just after that lady busted in there. That's when I called Buster and when he didn't answer, decided I better check things out."

Mary said, "That was probably her, his hooker. She talked to me for a minute. I decided I wasn't going through with it and was leaving. I got outside the inner door and she was standing there smoking. She said something about not intruding on my territory or something like that. She even asked me if I wanted to come to Chicago and work for her."

"Seriously," Marla said, "so she thought you were working the bar as a prostitute. She must have been the girl Scales was supposed to hook up with. What did you say to her, like, how much do you charge, something like that?"

"I didn't say anything, I kind of forgot how I was dressed. It scared me, so I went back in and then decided to go ahead and sit next to Dr. Scales. That's when Mrs. Ringwald and the rest of them recognized me."

"I wonder who the lady was that was beating on him."

Mary responded, "I think it was his wife."

"Well, that kind of blows the picture thing." Marla shrugged, "Oh well, it was a good idea. Wanna go get a burger?"

CHAPTER 34

"I still can't believe Mary Good is a prostitute. I know she's been hanging around with that Todd girl, but, come on, to go from a shoeless waif that couldn't put a full sentence together to a prostitute with mesh stockings and a leather skirt, come on," Rowena said staring at the TV without watching.

Jerry took a pull on his Leinie's and pulled the lever on the recliner sitting up, "Yeah, that's strange alright. What about the size of that dildo. Where do you suppose she got that?"

Ignoring that comment, Rowena asked, "Did you see the guy taking the pictures?"

"Yeah," Jerry replied, now a little more interested, "where'd he come from. You don't think he's from the paper or something."

"Not unless the Messenger's hiring motorcycle gang members. That's what has me totally confused. You put all of this stuff together and none of it makes any sense….. Jim meeting a student that has transformed herself into a prostitute; Jim's wife showing up when the mysterious rendezvous was supposed to be a secret; some gangbanger just happens to have a camera and starts taking pictures; it just doesn't make sense."

"Hey," Jerry said, "you've got the whole weekend to ponder this. The big question is, what's he gonna do Monday. You think he'll fire you?"

"What do you think, of course he'll fire me, and Lupinski, and probably sue Cardy. You're probably the only one that's in the clear."

Jerry took another pull on the Leinie's. "It was good while it lasted. Sure glad we didn't buy that house though; we'd be screwed without your check."

"Man, nothing bothers you, does it? I may be waitressing at the Kountry Kitchen next week and as long as you can afford another case of Leinenkugel, you're fine."

Jerry cranked the recliner back and put his arm behind his head and said, "Love you too, babe."

*

Jim Scales drove around the curve following the dogleg of the number ten fairway approaching his house with his cell phone at his ear listening for the twentieth time to the computer generated message on Cinderella's answering system. "Pleeeeease Cinderella, call me back, I need you......" He pulled the phone away from his ear as his driveway came into view. The upstairs window was open and clothes were strewn over the front yard, hanging on the bushes, with some still hanging in the window. He stopped in the middle of the street just in time to see a few pair of shoes come shooting out like they were being spit from a canon.

Damn, he thought, *those look like my new Ferragamo's, they cost me a grand, this woman is nuts.* He looked across the street and saw his neighbors, Ralph and Edna Strongbow, staring at the mess and then pointing at him, like he should do something. Realizing the futility of the situation, he did a U-turn and headed back up the street, deciding to retreat to the bar at the country club.

*

Randy Lupinski helped Father Cardone up the steps of the parsonage only to be met at the door by Mildred Tanner, her arms crossed on her chest with a look of displeasure that could melt an iceberg in winter.

"What's going on here?" She asked, not extending a hand to help prop up the rotund Priest.

"He may have had one too many," Lupinski answered sheepishly.

"One too many what?"

"He likes beer with jack chasers; at least he drank 'em like he did."

"And who are you, may I ask?"

"Randall Lupinski, I work for the community college."

"So, you meet in a bar, or what?"

"Could we get him inside? I don't think I can hold him much longer."

223

Mildred blew out a breath and looped her arm under Cardone's, "Come on, get him in on the couch."

"Iss it time for mass? I'll haf one more beer, ann maybe a cookie," Cardone slurred as they maneuvered him to the couch. He was snoring before they could turn to sit in the other chairs.

"Okay," Mildred said, "give me the whole story, and don't leave anything out in case I have to cover some tracks."

Randy spilled the whole story of the intervention gone terribly wrong and the resulting police interrogation.

"Well, as long as no one got arrested," Mildred said, talking more to herself than Lupinski, "at least that's good. It was over in the Falls, so not too many witnesses, at least that would know him. No pictures, anything like that." She noticed Lupinski shirk at the mention of pictures and immediately sensed a problem. "There weren't any pictures, *were there*?"

"Well, there was this guy, he wasn't with us; kind of a rough looking guy, you know, a lot of tattoos, big and bald. As soon as the commotion started I saw him jump up and start taking pictures. Then when the police showed up he was gone."

Mildred stared at Lupinski with a look that could draw sweat to the brow of a gorilla. "So," she said slowly and deliberately, "let me get this straight, you find out this Dr. Scales is meeting with a prostitute, even though it was supposed to be on the QT......, wasn't you or anyone else you know of set it up......., and then his wife comes in and starts beating on him, with a giant penis by the way, and coincidently, there's a candid camera guy there to catch all the action. I got that right?"

"Well, yeah, I guess that's about it."

224

"Mr. Lupinski, didn't you tell me you have a master's degree?"

"Well, almost, I still have........."

"Oh well," Mildred interrupted throwing up her hands, "that explains the fact that you couldn't see this was a total entrapment. You haven't finished your master's thesis yet, *that must be why you are so freaking stupid and naive.*"

Lupinski squirmed a little and tried to defend himself. "Father Cardone didn't see it coming either."

"*He's a Priest,* He doesn't have to be smart, he just has to be pure and dignified." She looked at him snoring on the couch and frowned. "Well, at least pure.

"Okay, Randall, here's what we, you and me, are going to do. First, we are going to find out who this photographer is. Then we are going to go find him and ask nicely if we can have the photos he took back. Then we are going to go find the hooker, this Good girl, and make sure she understands she needs to forget this ever happened."

"I don't think I want to get involved, I mean, further involved......"

"You *what,* you don't want to get involved; you're in up to your earlobes mister. Maybe that's why you didn't hear me say we, you and me are going to straighten this mess out. You started it, you and I are going to finish it." Mildred stood and looked at Cardone, "He'll be fine for the next few hours. Let's go."

"Go where?"

Mildred groaned, "Back to the motel, the scene of the crime. Are you really this......, forget it, let's go."

*

They pulled into the parking lot of the Best Western and the side entrance now displayed the lighted neon sign, *Twilight Lounge*. Mildred climbed out, her flowered dress and cardigan sweater not exactly timely attire for the night bar crowd.

"I'll stay here and watch the car," Lupinski said.

"Get your sorry butt out and let's go, it's getting late."

The room was nearly empty, only two patrons sitting at the bar and one booth occupied by a couple deep in romantic conversation. Mildred and Randy took seats at the bar.

"That the same bartender that was here this afternoon?" Mildred whispered.

"Yeah, I think."

The bartender quit washing glasses and walked down in front of them. "Hi folks, what can I get you?" He looked particularly long at Lupinski and then said, "You were one of them that was here this afternoon," he laughed, "man what a show that was."

Mildred interrupted the levity in her overbearing direct manner. "That's why we're here, looking for the bald guy that took the pictures; you know him?"

The bartender lost his smile and threw his bar towel over his shoulder. "Never saw him before."

Mildred turned to Lupinski, "Give me twenty dollars."

"What for?"

"Just give it to me."

Lupinski fished around in his wallet, looking through the ones to find a twenty.

226

Mildred laid the twenty on the bar. "Refresh your memory?"

The bartender rubbed his chin and looked up. "It's starting to come back to me but it's still a little foggy."

"Give him another twenty," Mildred ordered.

"Now just a minute," Lupinski objected, "This isn't right. Why do I have to be the one...."

Mildred turned her hard stare toward Lupinski and he pulled his wallet back out and started fishing again. This time it took a little longer but he found his last twenty folded behind a credit card.

The bartender palmed the other twenty and said, "His name's Buster, don't know his last name. He's a bouncer at *Bare Essentials* down the street."

Mildred looked at Lupinski, "You know where that is?"

"Well, yeah, that's Lisa Calmwater's club."

"Who is Lisa Calmwater?"

Lupinski cringed a little, "She teaches at the school."

"I should have known, let's go."

*

The parking lot of *Bare Essentials* was full and Lupinski had to squeeze between two mud covered pickup trucks with tractor sized tires. Trying to get out proved difficult and left a large mud stain on his Armani jacket. Mildred was out and marching toward the entrance while Lupinski tried to brush the mud off his coat.

Mildred waited for him at the front door that displayed a large sign declining entrance to anyone under twenty one and anyone else the club management found offensive. In addition, there was a twenty dollar cover charge and a three drink minimum.

Mildred said, "Let's go."

"I don't have another twenty dollars," Lupinski protested.

"You won't need it. Just point to the bald guy you think took the pictures." Mildred opened the door and charged in.

It wasn't difficult to find Buster; he stood next to a ticket cage just inside the door. She turned to Lupinski, "That him?"

"Yeah, I think so."

Mildred shook her head in disgust and marched over to Buster. "You Buster?" she yelled over the blasting music.

Buster looked at her and laughed, "Yeah, why....., one of your kids in here looking at titties?"

Mildred reached up and grabbed one of Buster's earrings and pulled, almost dragging him toward the front door. Lupinski opened the door and watched in amazement.

Outside, Buster grabbed Mildred's arm and said, "Hey bitch, who you think you are?"

"Right now, I'm your best friend, but that could change in a hurry." Mildred put the fingers on her right hand in the peace sign in front of Buster and pointed at her own eyes. "Are you looking at me Buster? Are you paying attention?"

"*What?*"

Lupinski slowly backed away into the shadow of the entrance alcove.

"Pay attention Buster, I'm only going to say this once. *Look at me Buster*, pay attention. This afternoon, you took some pictures in the bar at the Best Western. I want those pictures. I don't want to argue, just get me the camera."

228

"What? Are you fucking nuts? Who are you? I'm not giving you anything. You're lucky I don't knock your teeth down your throat."

"Buster, you're not paying attention." Once again she pointed at her eyes. "Look at me Buster, pay attention. Like I said, give me the camera, we'll erase the pictures, and we'll leave."

"Who are you? This isn't funny anymore, lady."

"Buster, listen to me. If you don't give me the camera, within a half hour I'll have fifty people standing out here with signs decrying the sinful nature of this establishment along with two cameras taking pictures of every deviant coming or going. What do you think Ms. Calmwater will think about that? And when she asks the nature of our discontent, I'll tell her that one of her prized employees likes to photograph her customers and use the pictures to extort money from them. I'll tell her that as I dial the Sheriff's office to report your little scam…… Are you paying attention *now,* Buster?"

"You're bluffing."

"Really? Randall, call Ms. Calmwater on your cell phone."

They both turned to see Lupinski standing in the shadows. He cautiously stepped out into the light.

"You're one of them that was at the bar today, I should'a knowed." Buster said spitting the words out.

Lupinski studdered, "I, I, it's nothing I did, I mean, I was just……"

Mildred interrupted, "He's a professor at the school with Lisa and they're close friends. Call her Randall."

Lupinski opened his mouth to say he had no idea what her phone number was but Buster beat him to the punch. "Why you want those pictures?"

229

"Buster, Buster, Buster," Mildred said condescendingly, "I know why you took those pictures. This is once you wasted your time. They'll be others, we both know that." She rested her hand on his shoulder, "Now go get the camera, like a good boy."

Buster gave Lupinski a scowl that said without words, *I won't forget this*, and turned and went back into the club.

Lupinski's knees were knocking and his hands shook so bad he had to cross his arms to hide them. "I can't believe you did that. You think he'll get the camera? I hope he doesn't come back out with a gun."

Mildred looked at Lupinski and said, "God help us if you are the next generation because you couldn't stand up to a sheep if it had its tail turned toward you."

CHAPTER 35

The semester opened with a shocking revelation for students and faculty. Rowena arrived early anticipating a busy day answering questions of new students and generally trying to get everyone up to speed. In the words of a sage Yankee catcher, it was de' ja vue all over again. A temporary sign tied to the former Super Value grocery sign that had been refaced with Hinkley Community College, Home of the Hooters, displayed a new name; University of The Americas, Hinkley Branch, for the Advancement of International Studies.

Rowena stood in the parking lot staring up at the temporary sign, attached with duct tape and rippling in the morning breeze. She couldn't help thinking about the morning she arrived for work at the Super Value and found the store closed and the building vacant. Her only thought was *He's done it to me again*, meaning Jim Scales pulling the rug out from under her. *At least this time, the building's not empty*.

She cautiously entered the building, noting everything pretty much looked the same, and walked the short distance to her office. It was intact, so she moved on down the hall to Dr. Scales's office. The door was ajar and the gold name plate had a piece of cardboard taped over it. Down one side were vertical chicken scratches and next to it printed in Sharpie smudges; Hung Su Chow, President. Rowena pushed the door open and peeked in.

A man behind the desk, obviously oriental, jumped up and bowed, sporting a giant smile. "Good morning, you must be Rorena Ringrald. Meester Scarels tore me you would be first to allive."

Rowena stared at the short man, speechless and then gathered enough thought to ask, "Where's Dr. Scales?"

"Meester Scarels no ronger work here. I take his place. We buy." Hung Su offered the broad smile again.

Rowena plopped down in the plush chair in from of the desk. "Who buy?"

"University of Americas, we buy. We big company, international, rook at internet." Hung Su pecked a few times on his keyboard and then turned the large monitor toward her. The screen was interactive displaying the name across the top with action pictures of students of all races in labs, in libraries, in student unions casually conversing, and of course working diligently on computers. "Home office in Shanghai."

"Shang who?"

"No, Shangjo far away from Shanghai. Shanghai important financial city."

Rowena rubbed her forehead, "I think I'm gonna be sick."

"No sick, never hear that city, Shanghai, it big city."

The Hinkley Messenger

HEADLINE: Community College Sold

By Line: Martin Red Redderson, Editor

The Hinkley Community College, a for profit junior college located in Hinkley was sold last week to another for profit educational giant, The University of The Americas, Inc. The corporation is domiciled in the state of Delaware but all indications are that it is wholly owned by a Chinese conglomerate located in Shanghai, China. The local college is now known as The University Of The Americas, Hinkley County Branch.

Terms of the sale are private, but the transaction had to be approved by the Community College Resource and Performance Board which is subject to the open public records Freedon of Information Act. The Messenger was able to secure terms of the sale that include $14,500,000 for 100% of the stock which was held by the Scales Family Trust plus other consideration in the form of consulting fees to be paid to Dr. James Scales over a 3 year contract. In addition, the new owner purchased the real estate that the school currently occupies from Roush Holdings, Inc. for $1,500.000.

Calls to Dr. Scales office were not returned. Calls to the home office of The University of the Americas in Shanghai were not returned as well. Attempted access to the Hinkley Community College web site automatically diverted to the web site of the University of the Americas.

The Hinkley Community College specialized in hands on training and had recently been awarded the opportunity to offer Associate Degree training in Business and finance. In addition, the college had recently entered into a long term contract through an outside vendor to offer an Associate degree via the internet and had been positioning its curriculum to offer Bachelor degrees once approved by CRAP.

The acquisition by The University of the Americas will elevate the community college to a fully accredited university offering associate and master degrees via the internet and on-site classes.

*

Lupinski sat at the counter of the Kountry Kitchen diner, sucking on a bitter cup of coffee and looking at the day old donut he had ordered. His stomach twisted at the thought of eating it. He had arrived at the school, ready to work his way through the new roster of students, knowing that only about half of the new recruits would show up and that they would most likely skip any assigned classes.

After the initial shock of the new sign and lack of the usual hustle bustle of new students high fiving and hanging around the pool tables and concession area, he had walked to his office to find the door locked and his personal key not functional. He walked to Dr. Scales office to find the smiling Chinaman who said, "You no work here anymore." His diatribe of questioning was ignored and he finally gave up and drove to the Kountry Kitchen.

He dialed Rowena's cell and got her answering service, "Rowena, this is Randy, what's going on? Have you talked to Scales? Did you get fired? Call me."

His cell phone chirped and the call screening said *Father Cardone.*

Mildred said, "Randall, is that you?"

Lupinski answered solemnly, "Yes, Miss Tanner, it's me."

"Pick me up in five minutes. Father Cardone has concluded morning mass and had his snack. He'll be resting for an hour. I want to talk to Mary Good."

"I don't know why I……,"

"Don't argue with me Randall, just be here in five minutes." She clicked off.

His phone chirped again.

"Randy, it's me, Rowena."

"What is going on? What's with the smiling Chinese guy, and the new sign?"

"I suppose you didn't read the Saturday Messenger."

"The Saturday what?"

Rowena sighed, regretting already what she was about to explain. She had only read the story after getting a copy that morning. After a lengthy repetition of the news article to Lupinski she continued, "The rumor I am getting is that by the end of this semester, there won't be any more classrooms, it will all be online. They are going to turn this building into their Midwest service office and computer center. Everything will be, how did he put it, in the clouds, or up in the sky, or something like that. Anyway, there won't be any faculty, at least working here."

"He got fourteen million?" After that piece of information, Lupinski had hardly heard the rest of the story.

"That's what the paper said. After the Accreditation review, and all the issues that were revealed at that meeting; the pony thing; the attendance records; and let's not forget the sick kids in the day care, that was a real winner; I figure Jim knew he was in trouble, maybe even under the gun to do something, and this sale was the answer."

"It was more than an answer, if you ask me, it was falling in a pit of slop and finding gold. By the way, Mildred Tanner, you know who I mean, anyway, she wants me to take her to see Mary Good, the girl you thought you saw at the bar." Lupinski waited for a response.

Rowena spoke with great suspicion in her voice, "Mildred, that's Father Cardone's maid, or something like that. What does she want with Mary Good?"

"I don't know, but you should have seen her in action with the skinhead guy that took the pictures at the bar. She's obviously pretty protective of the Father, I mean, she did a number on that guy and got all the pictures erased."

Rowena's head was spinning, "*What,* I thought that was over, and now she wants to find the Good girl?"

"I'm supposed to pick her up, like, ten minutes ago."

Rowena was thinking outloud, "She's probably here, at the school, in the daycare."

"Okay, we'll be there in ten minutes," Lupinski ended the call.

"Wait, wait," but it was too late.

*

Mildred, Lupinski and Rowena found Mary and Marla sitting on the bench next to the concession machines, talking quietly.

Marla looked up and saw the three approaching and said, "Uh oh, let me handle this." Marla crossed her legs, stiffened her back and gave the three adults a solid grin as they approached.

Lupinski started the conversation. "Marla Todd and May Good, meet Mildred Tanner. You both know Mrs. Ringwald."

Marla didn't waste any time. "What's with the new school name? This another scam to get the students to contribute to somebody's retirement fund?"

Mildred looked at Mary, "Mary, look at me, I'm not here to do anything except find out the facts."

Marla interrupted, "Facts about what?"

Mildred ignored Marla. "Mary, pay attention, were you at the Best Western Thursday afternoon when Father Cardone was there? That's all I want to know."

"No she wasn't there," Marla blurted out, "and it's none of your business anyway."

"Mary, look at me," Mildred repeated, "I want to hear it from you."

Marla opened her mouth to protest but Mary held up her hand. "I was there."

237

Rowena said, "I thought it was you, but, the way you were dressed."

Everyone relaxed a little and Mary proceeded to tell the whole truth and nothing but the truth, much to Marla's continued protest. She laid out the plan as developed by Marla and then described the last minute changes in detail. Her only defense was she was trying to protect Marla from being recognized, the only friend she had, but then added a caveat that her concern for Marla was no excuse for what she did.

When she was done Mildred bent down and placed a hand on her knee. "Young lady, I see nothing wrong with what you did in defense of your friend. In fact, it was quite admirable, somewhat illegal, but quite admirable."

Marla reached over and hugged Mary, "Hats, I don't know what I would do without you."

CHAPTER 36

Father Cardone concluded his short sermon during Sunday Mass by making a special announcement. "Fellow parishioners, I'm pleased to announce today that the Saint Matthew Barromeo will establish a scholarship fund for present and future youth of our parish. Without going into great detail about the origins of the fund, I can announce that the endowment that will perpetuate this endeavor was gifted by our fellow Knight of Columbus James Scales through his family trust. Dr. Scales couldn't be with us today, but is no doubt here in spirit.

"The scholarship fund will be named the Scales Family Scholarship Fund and I am proud to announce today the first two recipients who were chosen by the donor. As we proceed, a committee will be selected to establish criteria for future awards on an annual basis.

"Our first recipient is a graduate of Hinkley High School and has started her post high school studies at the University of the Americas, formerly known as Hinkley Community College, and will study biological science at the University of Illinois and intends to pursue a career in Cosmetology sciences. May I present Marla Todd, daughter of George and Ruth Todd."

A raucous round of applause erupted in the sanctuary as Marla approached the Alter. Marla wore a knee length black skirt and long sleeve blouse buttoned at the neck. Nary a tattoo was visble and her broad smile revealed the tongue ring was also gone. Marla's parents reveled in the lime light, standing as she left the pew.

"Our second recipient is a graduate of the Central Mennonite School and, as well, started her college studies at the University of the Americas. May I present Mary Good, daughter of Ralph and Audrey Good."

Once again, a loud response applause came and Mary stepped up to the altar. She, as well, wore a long black skirt and white blouse. She wore her traditional hair net bonnet proudly and grasp Marla's hand as she took her position. Ralph and Audrey Good did not attend, expressing their, at least Ralph's disrespect for the Catholic ceremony.

"Mary Good intends to study primary education at the University of Illinois and intends to become a primary school teacher. We can only hope she will select one of our fine Catholic Parochial institutions."

*

The mass ended and Marla and Mary stood in line with Father Cardone shaking hands as the congregation exited, each congregant expressing congratulations with each shake.

240

Bringing up the rear, Mildred Tanner stood before the two girls, her hands clasped in front, same dull expression giving no clue as to her demeanor. "Well…., I guess we accomplished something after all, didn't we?"

Cardone shook the final hand and turned to join the conversation but instead got a stern look from Mildred and walked away.

"Ladies, you just don't know how proud I am of you both. You stood up and faced the enemy, and won. Not many your age would have taken the initiative, no matter how……, well, I won't go there, but I'm proud of you both."

Mary said, "This wouldn't have happened if not for you Miss Tanner. We both know Dr. Scales would never have done this without your……., well, I won't go there."

The comment drew a laugh from Mildred, the first time either girl, or for that matter, Father Cardone who was standing a few feet away, had ever seen her laugh.

EPILOGUE

J im Scales sat at his desk, a panoramic view of Lake Michigan to his back and an expansive, walnut paneled office decorated in purple hues and shag carpet before him. The golden inscription on the outer door of the suite of offices declared *CJ Escort Service, The Royal Treatment is Our Minimum Standard.*

Cindy Scales, aka Cinderella, aka Valerie Smanski Scales, sat at her desk in the next office perusing the latest issue of *Mademoiselle* and contemplating an afternoon trip to *Saks.* The evening appointment book was at capacity, including three members of the New York Giants who were in town for the Sunday game.

Jim pressed the intercom button, "Cinderella, my darling, how about lunch today at the Hiatt?"

"My Jimmy, always trying to impress me. *No,* I don't want to have lunch, I have plans." The line went dead.

*

Rowena Ringwald used her chop sticks to push around the sashimi California roll topped with squid roe attempting to give some credibility to her effort to eat the appetizer, not wanting to offend the honored guest at their luncheon meeting. Hung Lo Chow sat next to her, gobbling his portion in anticipation of the main course, while continuing to show great interest in the muted conversation with their guest in Chinese.

Mot Su Wang, CEO of Wang International, parent company of the University of the Americas, sitting next to Chow, was making a national tour of the school's facilities, concentrating on expense management with a power point presentation emphasizing human resource payroll control; in other words, how to conduct business and increase profit without any employees.

Chow considered himself a master at expense management, having cut payroll by eighty percent in his first six months on the job. Rowena had no idea why she still had a job, other than Chow had not figured out how to operate the office without at least one employee who spoke English. The only faculty member still in good standing was Lisa Calmwater, who by virtue of some after hours extracurricular activities with Chow and his free door pass to *Bare Essentials*, had made the necessary moves to hold control over her employment. Her duties were limited to managing the tournament schedule for the Hooters eight ball pool team and making sure the outside sand lot volley ball court was in good repair.

The following semester, after the transition of ownership, all classes were converted to online access with the science lab converted to a bank of computer monitors for those students who didn't own a computer and still wanted to complete a

243

class. This change left the building empty with exception of occasional pool tournaments or student's parents searching for someone to listen to their complaints.

The main course of the luncheon, prepared by Wang's personal chef and served by his personal female attendants consisted of sea bass smothered in what appeared to Rowena to be weeds, maybe dandelions, but were described by Chow as sea grass, surrounded by round brown things. Rowena made the mistake of asking Chow what they were and he provided a big tooth filled smile and said "Flied caterpillars," as he popped one in his big mouth and chewed, brown goo seeping down his chin.

Rownena threw her hand over her mouth but could not hold back the rush of vomit that sprayed the table. She looked up to see the partial remains of her breakfast splattered on Wang's handmade in Hong Cong shirt and silk tie.

Chow said, "Hory mackerel that stinks."

Lisa Calmwater, who was sitting on the other side next to Wang and had been rubbing his leg under the table, was used to the stench of vomit, something her club smelled like every morning at three AM, so she reached over and dabbed at Wang's shirt and tie with a napkin and said, "It's okay baby."

Wang said in Chinese "Stupid Americans," waved his hands to the attendants, "we leave," and grabbed Lisa's hand and headed for his limo.

4 YEARS LATER

Mary Good walked down a long isle of pallets laden with boxes ready for shipping. Women, dressed in floor length dresses and lace hair bonnets, worked at individual stations monitoring machines that spit out labels to be applied to specific boxes traveling down conveyor belts. The warehouse shipped an average of five thousand parcels a day.

Since graduating from the University of Illinois, Mary managed the manufacturing and wholesale distribution side of *EMs Cosmetics.* The original name was *M & M Cosmetics*, but a trade name infringement suit brought by Hershey Chocolates under the argument that M & M Chocolate Covered Candies could be considered useful in facial cosmetology, especially if the user wanted to grow more acne, required a name change. Marla and Mary decided on *EMs*, a play on the M & M name.

Marla headed up the research and development side of the company working in the old biology lab. In her senior year at the University of Illinois, completing a research paper on the effects of acidic astringents on tattoos, she discovered a cosmetic treatment that over time disintegrated the color pigments of tattoos and eventually made them translucent, or just a mild discoloration that could be easily covered with a mild makeup.

The two girls presented Marla's discovery to several large cosmetic companies and had offers ranging from an entry level job to a sizable offer to buy the formula out right.

Instead they sought help from an old friend, Dr. Jim Scales. Unfortunately, Dr. Jim and his new wife fell into disfavor with the Chicago and Federal authorities and after being arrested for running a prostitution ring and an additional charge resulting from a federal warrant for tax fraud, ended up serving modest sentences in the Federal penitentiary in Omaha. Dr. Jim only served twenty months since it was his first offense while Cinderella received five years due to her four prior offenses for prostitution and three priors for tax evasion. They divorced while incarcerated and Dr. Jim returned to Hinkley upon release.

Fortunately for Dr. Jim, his family trust was impenetrable by the feds so he retained sizable wealth heading into his retirement years. The opportunity to invest in *EMs Cosmetology* gave him pleasure and gave the girls the resources to start their business. Jim Scales occupied his old office in the front of the building with a gold plated insignia on the door, *Dr. James Scales, CFO.*

During Scales stint in the slammer and the girls' undergraduate education, the *University of the Americas* came under the scrutiny of the United States Department of Education for student loan fraud, conspiracy to commit interstate mail fraud and two Hundred and twenty seven other criminal offenses. After thirty six months of investigation, the indictments came down from the U.S. Attorney General's office, but all of the named defendants had fled the country back to China. The real estate holdings of the bankrupt company were confiscated and sold at auction, giving Jim Scales the opportunity to purchase the *Super Value; Hinkley Community College; University of the Americas* building for a song and lease it back to *EMs Cosmetology.*

Rowena Ringwald, Director of Human Resources, recruited employees primarily from the local Amish and Mennonite communities, giving young women the opportunity to learn a trade and a reasonable living. In addition, the company sponsored scholarships for any employee wishing to continue their education at an approved state or private institution, for profit schools excluded.

THE END

Books by Craig Sullivan

Hinkley County

The First State Bank
and (dis) Trust

Breaking Wind

School Daze
The Hinkley Community
College Chronicles

www.ingramcontent.com/pod-product-compliance
Lightning Source LLC
LaVergne TN
LVHW091250080426
835510LV00007B/190